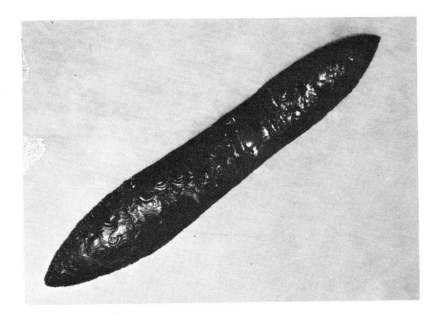

The distinctive ceremonial blade originated deep in the past ages of Indian life. An amazing and beautiful work of art, the famous blade plays a highly significant role in the tracing of primitive (western) movements.

The one pictured above was rescued as the flood of 1964 toppled banks containing the skeletal remains of these ancient people. It is 12-3/8 inches long; 2-3/8 inches wide at the large end; 1-7/8 inches wide at both the center and small end, and 5/8 of an inch thick. The centers of these blades are usually smaller than either end. Held by their centers, they are wielded in an impressive ceremonial dance, ends flashing in the sun.

The Yurok Indians possess a number of these unique blades, and use them yet only for special ceremonial occasions. (Gold Hill Site.)

ISBN 0-912906-02-2

SILENT ARROWS
Earl F. Moore

Indian Lore and Artifact Hunting
Illustrator: Juanita Anderson

MUSE PRESS, OREGON, LTD.
Trail, Oregon

June 27, 1973

Mrs. Barbara J. Muse
Muse Press, Oregon Ltd.
Trail, Oregon 97541

Dear Mrs. Muse:

I do indeed remember the visit to Mr. Moore's Museum and the wonderful opportunity I had to talk with him. I am pleased to learn that a book is finally being published by him since I feel he is one of the very rare self-made scholars that has contributed so much to our understanding of the Indian People. We have come to know and appreciate these Native Americans through the dedication and learned expertise of those few like Earl Moore. His warm, wonderful personality, brightness and enthusiasm, are apparent as he recounts the many details of his findings which are so carefully catalogued and even sketched as they are prepared for display.

Please convey my very best to Mr. Moore and to his family. I sincerely hope that his great collection will ultimately find a home where it can be displayed and appreciated by the thousands of people who may gain a better knowledge of the history of the land in which we live. I hope to have an opportunity to see his text once it is published and you may quote freely from this letter if you so desire.

Sincerely yours,

Paul F. Romberg
President of California State University
San Francisco, California

PFR:ec

DEDICATION

I humbly dedicate *Silent Arrows* to my beloved family and good friends, who have shared with me a most gracious span of years.

Earl F. Moore

EDITOR'S NOTE

In an effort to preserve the authentic, down to earth wisdom of seven full decades, the editorial pencil has remained pretty well unsharpened.

Mr. Moore's education as an archaeologist was gained mostly in the field, under the open skies he loved; and the evidence of his expertise in this field is both overwhelming and publicly acknowledged.

This book is Mr. Moore. Because of that, the scientific data could not possibly be separated from the personal approach. This is as it should be; for in him the scientist is inextricably interwoven with the man.

His dedication to his work; his devotion to his friends; and his genuine respect and love for the ancient peoples of this land and their descendants literally seep forth throughout its pages.

Silent Arrows, then, is a combination of scientific text, personal (and expert) viewpoints, and invaluable, practical advice to both amateur and professional archaeologists.

Yet most of all, because of its flavor, it stands as a testimonial to its writer; a rare and uplifting glimpse into the soul of a good man.

We are proud to have edited, illustrated and published *Silent Arrows.*

Barbara Muse
Juanita Anderson

© Juanita Anderson
7.7

FOREWORD

The period of time centering around the year of my birth, 1895, was one still clinging to, and living by pioneer influences. I found those same years to be the decisive ones in the rise and fall of various boyhood ambitions. However, it soon became evident that I was leaning heavily toward the study of our Indian neighbors, and even then my search was under way for Stone Age artifacts. This lifelong archaeological career has been maintained to the current year, 1973, and hopefully will continue for many more.

Early in life I found the range lands of Klamath, Lake and Harney Counties to be a vast reservoir of lively western history. From those open spaces of untamed freedom, I set course on future ambitions.

Aged Indian acquaintances were very much instrumental in shaping up these plans; for their knowledge of times long past fit nicely into the pattern. White pioneer ranchers had much to relate of the western expansion. Therefore, it is not as the least of my possessions that I hold the confidences of those remarkable and trusting people of the range; nor has it escaped my mind to thank them, regardless of blood, for the helping hand along the way. I conscientiously say that I am thankful for having lived a good portion of my life in an atmosphere of western hospitality.

Thus, in 1903, at the age of eight, on the upper waters of the Sprague River, Klamath County, Oregon, I started my present day Stone Age collection consisting of over 14,000 relics.

Our Sprague River Indian friends and neighbors were of Klamath and Modoc families. Most senior members, and many of the following generation proudly upheld their native ancestry; and being so willing to talk of former habitations, I gathered from them an enormous amount of information concerning Indian artifacts. These person to person, live and reliable confirmations on the usage of stone implements, tools, weapons and natural cache locations shall not be lost to future interested parties so long as this and like books go to press in an effort to preserve the fast dwindling sources.

While individual viewpoints are often considered personal innovations, actual field verifications, in most cases, eliminates the chance of misrepresentation. The bridging of gaps, by tracing family lineage back to frontier blood, becomes especially important in correctly identifying a uniquely designed relic. Old battle grounds, tribal sites and natural hunting and fishing areas were the fields from which I've gathered a large portion of my extensive collection, and verified their usage.

Historically speaking, we of the early 1900's were blessed with the rare opportunity of enjoying visits and fireside chats with some of the Indian elders who had survived the dismemberment of tribal frontiers, beginning with the early and mid-1800's. As a youth I was deeply impressed, or perhaps more aptly stated, unusually vulnerable to the live accounts of the progression of their native wild life to the storm swept crossroads of the white man. This Indian history, so graciously narrated to me by the old "true bloods" I had grown to love and admire, was by and large the background that served me well on many, many future digging operations.

Readers may anticipate frequent references to the rare and unusual discoveries now on display for public viewing. This book is predominantly reenactments of a number of actual field operations; a factor prevailing expressly for an inspirational effect upon the serious minded, coming archaeologist.

The cold, primitive campsite has a last duty to perform. Every arrowhead, spearhead, blade or other artifact conveys a special message from the Indian's sacred earth; all his by right of birth.

This writing is actually the outgrowth of the arrowhead enthusiasm of 1903. The two hundred photographs show the outstanding finds in my long hunt, adding live and colorful emphasis to prominent subjects such as regional breakdowns, campsite study, the prehistoric peoples involved, and chosen suggestions leading to better hunting.

A western atmosphere of originality is evidenced in a number of trailside briefs, but that is the way I saw it, and lived it.

Although authentic, and standing on present day conclusions concerning Stone Age people and their stone crafts, histories will continue to be written and rewritten, as long as later archaeological discoveries reveal more of the previously unknown.

As these fine old history bearing artifacts are unearthed, many are subjected to over-ambitious conclusions, theories, legendary hearsay and personal versions of a thrilling story. The true value of this primitive work is lost by such maneuvering. Even so, of late years miscontrued facts have been detected and corrected.

Numerous methods used in the removal and preservation of age old, perishable relics are discussed in the following, but I will say most methods must be devised "on the spot" to meet existing conditions and the nature of the material. I have spent up to three days in a single cave or deep pit before coming up with a successful method of intact removal.

The text also stresses the importance of a prestudy of regional geography, prior to an extensive operation. Tribal differences in customs and needs for survival were due primarily to climatic conditions, locations, altitudes, sources of food, etc. Those new in this field are urged to give a deal of thought to the matter, while remembering that a systematic approach alerts the collector to tools and implements most likely to be found in a given area. Campsite kitchen midden deposit, for instance, shows tribal needs are fairly well established by the presence or absence of certain artifact material, such as heavy game heads, bird points or fishing implements.

My book embraces a wide range of Indian works, from Stone Age findings associated with B.C. Archaic tribesmen, to the 19th century subjugation and transformation of the wild Indian into a new society. Many dim trails into the prehistoric past are yet to be restored; a restoration to which my outstanding collection should lend major support. Artifacts of primitive man are numerous, and ofttimes conflicting in supposed tribal placement. The tributaries of his existence, measured in millennial years give rise to sincere debate; but any constructive difference in opinion is welcomed as a personal right.

The old full blood Indian acquaintances of Klamath County, and their ancestral Stone Age cultures have been the inspiration behind my achievements. Because of them, I have tried to discharge what I feel and have been told was a duty; hopefully a partial fulfillment of archaeological expectation and public demand.

As the preliminary compiling of records and field notes progressed, I found it nearly impossible to scrap all humorous happenings on the trail. They are included mainly in response to the younger reader's trend of interest; a bit of live approach to the text documentation. A poll, taken among hundreds of visitors to our Indian museum, showed a nearly unanimous acclaim for this type of book in presenting the archaeological material, much of which was discovered and retrieved under the most unusual circumstances.

Seven decades in this Stone Age research can uncover many question marks.

Individual concepts of personal involvement in the study of Indian life and artifact research may well be short of scientific levels, but in all sincerity of purpose, and to the best of my knowledge, I have prepared the following in hopes of establishing a number of heretofore unknown, or bypassed field procedures leading to more rewarding efforts.

While yet in contact with things and people of the closing years of the 1800's and early 1900's, we have at last recognized the urgency of getting this once in a lifetime information into print. However or whatever disposition made by various writers, it has formed the impressive and essential background for this latest book on relic hunting.

As a final foreword note, the leading chapter, "My Friend The Indian" was implemented expressly as a means of briefly reviving recollections of those native people responsible for the relics we seek. If by some measure this writing has left a better understanding of our frontier Indian predecessors and their amicable twentieth century descendants, then the work has attained its primary goal.

Author

Chapter I
MY FRIEND THE INDIAN

CHAPTER I

MY FRIEND, THE INDIAN

Throughout my lifelong search for Stone Age artifacts, colorful relationships with old Indian friends have added a certain and significant richness to the findings. Having conversed with Indians who were seniors in the early 1900's, their valuable, first-hand information on artifact usage is shared with readers not so fortunate as I, in the following chapters.

Though that generation of Klamaths and Modocs in Klamath County was approaching their time of rest, their traits, knowledge, cultures and memories of ancestors would not be lost, if I could but record them. These departing tribal members had mostly abandoned their Stone Age arts, but we are grateful for their laconic descriptions of Indian life three or four generations previous.

As a boy, I was unusually attentive at conversations between my parents and Indian people. Repeatedly, I broke in with long lists of new questions. Though seemingly not too important at the time, notes jotted down from such meetings were referred to many times later, proving to be prime factors in my future exploratory work. Grandparents of my ancient friends, living before Lewis and Clark barged down the Columbia, had passed down so very much information. All possible use was made of my rare opportunity to hear their related stories of Indian frontiers and free roaming days.

So it is that we appreciate the last voices from descendants of western tribes, once living in the hereditary, untamed spaces. These valuable conversations are highly stressed by me, for verbal contact with the period of history in which the Indian was frustrated, floundering and suffering from the inroads of the white invaders is rapidly diminishing.

Stained pages of western occupation have left our own generation little choice in evaluating the severe subjugation of the Plains Indians and Pacific coastal tribes by military forces. It is our sad privilege to travel western highways and read the historic roadside monuments dedicated to those who fought. The overall picture revealed is one of bloody conflict on most Indian frontiers.

Villages on the prairie lands of the Dakotas and in Montana were ravaged and destroyed by merciless wars. The vast Sioux complex was left starving, bleeding and scattered into weak, roving bands; pitiful remnants of tribes once proud and powerful. Breezes over the rolling plains ceased to carry the far cry of battle from Cheyenne, Sioux and lesser tribes. Buffalo by the running herd, or by tens of thousands were slaughtered by white invaders. Pulled from the carcasses by horses, the hides brought one and a half dollars each, while the red man's precious meat was left to rot. The white man's primary motive was the money, but the secondary purpose proved to be that of starving the Indian into submission.

The famous and proudly worn eagle feather headdresses disintegrated with fallen warriors, while squaws mourned the loss of families; especially their young braves who failed to return from battle fronts. Wolves prowled and sniffed the skeletal remains of human and animal alike, while devastation continued to roll westward.

Incidentally, in 1916, '17, and the early part of '18, I rode for horses and cattle, employed by a southeast Montana rancher. It was most inspiring to ride over old Sioux trails, and through vast areas of buffalo slaughter grounds. One of my riding sidekicks was a half-blood Sioux. His mother was none other than Ekalaka, a full-blood Sioux. for whom the small town of Ekalaka was named. From the saddle "on the spot" observations were made of those sad reminders left by the white occupants of lands once teeming with unmarred and unmolested life in the tepee village. The endless, wild, realistic atmosphere almost led one into the false expectation of seeing an Indian encampment just around that next chalk butte; but only miles of uninhabited desolation met the eye. Personal sympathetic tendencies toward our Indian people mounted to new heights within me.

At that time, the battle of the Little Big Horn was but forty years distant; a very short span, even in a man's lifetime. Substituting vague thoughts for fact, the decades seemed to fade; for Indian paint pony blood was definitely flowing yet in the veins of many cayuses we gathered for eastern markets. The long, running hours of dust eating afforded an opportune time and setting to reflect upon Montana's dark days of Indian wars.

Today's limitations stem from knowing those famous personalities and great war chiefs involved at the Little Big Horn solely through historic writings. Speculations, criticism and attempts to minimize the many "ifs" cannot erase even one of those last bloody hours. However, well founded personal viewpoints can often lead one to a reassessment of overlooked issues.

The (to me) outstanding book, "My Friend the Indian" by Colonel James McLaughlin, certainly sharpens the outsider's awareness. United States Indian Inspector, and Agent of Indian Affairs for fifty-two years, this man preserved for future America complete and authentic record of his personal involvement in the Cheyenne and Sioux subjugation, and their subsequent rehabilitation into white circles. He knew the village families and tribal chieftains by name, was a friend to most, and was openly considerate of the wild Indian's traits. Their views and hair trigger characteristics that often led to bloodshed were completely understood and sympathized with by him.

Throughout those trying years of carrying out government orders, (often contrary to better judgment) acting as peacemaker and mediator between hostile tribes and government agencies, Mr. McLaughlin maintained prestige and dignity by his friendly relationships, wisdom and coolness in council, horsemanship admirable even to the Indian, and a willingness to accept any physical challenge on the red man's terms.

In the book he emphasized his special relationship with the powerful Chief Gall, a Hunkpapa Sioux who took over full command of red allied forces at the Little Big Horn. In later conversation with Gall, McLaughlin was given full details of the strategic moves that resulted in the surrounding and massacre of the entire command of General George Custer on June 25th, 1876. Mr. McLaughlin, a great humanitarian, was a strong advocate of truth, honesty and square dealings with the suspicious Indian; virtues that peaceably settled more inflamed disputes than gunfire. Do read the book.

No distinct line of demarkation exists between the historic and the prehistoric. Yet we do recognize that the overlapping began when white men first invaded Indian tribal lands, and history began to record the lives of the natives.

More knowledge comes from Indians whose ancestors, and great numbers of those were living at the time of their "discovery", had existed in the prehistoric ages. This was of great importance to the first traders, trappers and exploring scouts. Amazed by what they saw and heard, their saddlebag notations eventually merged into our written western histories.

The opening of new territories west of the Rocky Mountains by Lewis and Clark started another wave of pioneer infiltration that was soon to disrupt the peaceable lives of the natives. The white explorers were thoroughly bewildered by the sight of so many tribes occupying the Columbia River Basin. Most impressive was the large number of tribes that gathered annually for prolonged trading festivals at centers like Celilo Falls. From far and near they came; bringing with them horses, trinkets, furs, deer hides and numerous other articles of trade value. Those living some distance from this great source of fish were especially keen to exchange their treasures for the highly palatable smoked salmon. To picture the magnitude of such annual festivities we might pause and look at the four thousand head of horses wrangled here for one such large-scale trade talk. Chieftains gathered to smoke in silence as they watched the wild dances around special fires. Indian women, as usual, were the work horses of the tribe; responsible for the preparation of food, smoking meats, gathering berries, and caring for the little papoose on her back. Yet, the overall picture of tribal life was one of happiness; a people content and free from the white man's interference.

Tommy Thompson, hereditary Chief of the Wy-am-pum people at Celilo, passed on to us a wealth of ancestral Indian history. He and his wife Flora were and are much beloved personalities by those who knew them — a monumental tribute to their lives. Their spiritual devotion is clearly expressed by Henry Thompson, son of the aged Chief. He says, *"Ours is one of the religions which the Creator has created, and it is well respected. This religion created for the red people is one of the oldest. Without the Bible, these people knew the word of worship which is respected by all nations."*

"These people " then, whose name meant "The people of the water echoing against the rocks" were the very ones Lewis and Clark observed that day, long ago.

The Lewis and Clark party found little war uneasiness among the newly discovered people, for they had, as yet, been uninformed of the complete subjugation of tribes beyond the big mountains to the east. Indian runners and scouts had brought in scattered reports from time to time, but there was plenty of land here for themselves and few white travelers. Furthermore, these white men had brought them steel knives and

16

tomahawks, blankets, and beautiful blue beads for nothing but a guarantee of safe passage through Indian country. The Indian little suspected the real issues that lay beneath this gaudy camouflage.

In fact, we gather from early articles, the first tribes contacted by white forerunners welcomed them with open arms, for the new men seemed friendly, peaceable and neighborly. Wild tribesmen were comparable to little children, as they toyed with shiny objects never before seen. The palefaces covered with long hair were equally amusing, and gave rise to unlimited tepee giggling among young squaws.

These same early pages have been our authority concerning the first transgressions by white men into tribal lands of the west, and a major portion strikes a chord of disapproval. The inland tribes of Oregon, Washington and the Columbia River complex were unsuspecting, caught off guard and completely vulnerable to the white man's oratory. When they did begin to feel the pressure of military strength, it was too late to do other than fight the enemy in small bands, retreat, and move farther back. It was said negotiations were going on around council fires with tribal leaders, but to the Indian these "pow wows" turned out to be little more than a bag of misrepresentations, one-sided treaties and broken promises. We of this period hardly stand as judges of governmental policy in the acquisition of new lands; yet our humanitarian principles rebel against the methods used. Unhealed wounds still smart from the sting of over-ambitious gunfire.

History also reveals that it was quite in keeping with military tactics to first open fire, and immediately thereafter press hard bargains upon remaining tribal members. Revengeful retaliation was the Indian's last recourse, and in this they were professional savages of the wild. This period left us many conflicting accounts of widespread destruction and depradations, but time has shown the cause was evidently in favor of the red man.

Half a century of bitter Indian wars followed the early 1800 period of friendly relationships (trading and maneuvering for future advantage) with tribal chieftains. Confused tribes were confronted with possible annihilation. Warriors in the open wilds filtered back from defeats, reorganized, avenged the loss of fallen ones and at the same time provided for families near starvation.

But when faced with the final ultimatum of moving onto reservation confines or surrendering to the military, the spirit died in the breasts of a tired, war-weary people. This drastic United States Government "reform" was surely the end of their free roaming birthright; nor would this be all. Restricted to small pieces of land, Indian pride deteriorated when forced to ask the invading enemy for things necessary to survival. Bitter resentment followed.

Though statistics show on paper that food, farm tools, breeding stock and seed grain were amply supplied to them, many Indian Chiefs insisted they could not keep their people from half starving on the small amounts. In desperation, outlaw leaders gathered into bands and broke from the reservation bounds only to be pursued, crushed

17

and disposed of by lead, a hangman's rope or imprisonment for life.

Today we read numerous accounts of bloody uprisings in the Indian's final bid for freedom that could only terminate in humiliating defeat. Superior United States military strength soon destroyed the core of resistance and forced Indian captives to watch public execution of their braves, as a policy of stamping out any smouldering plans for another break.

Those interested in the closing days of Indian frontiers should, as a duty, read about Captain Jack (Kientepoos), Chief and Leader of the Modoc outbreak from the Klamath reservation in southern Oregon. In the lava beds, just south of the Oregon-California border, brave warriors and families risked all in a showdown battle for government acknowledgment of one concession. They simply wished to return to their Lost River homes. Captain Jack had repeatedly stated to the commanding personnel at Fort Klamath, Oregon and Yreka, California that all he wanted for himself and his people was to go back to their homes and live in peace.

There, in the caverns of volcanic lava formations Captain Jack, Schonchin, Scarface Charley, Shacknasty and forty-nine other noble warriors made their brave and notorious stand against inconceivable odds.

For a time they outmaneuvered, and then fought to a finish a thousand United States troops.

Fully aware of the depredations and killings, Captain Jack nonetheless maintained to the hour he, Black Jim, Boston Charley and Schonchin were hanged that he saw no bad blood in his heart.

The generation following the 1873 Modoc War was approximately that of my parents, and several acquaintances were very helpful in translating to us the things a few older members found difficult to express.

Without question, I easily lined up on the side of the Indian while quite young. The years still find myself and my wife making annual trips to visit Indian friends, a few of whom have passed the one hundred and five year mark.

I truly believe that an aged Indian neighbor lady, on the Klamath reservation, gave us more understanding of the trials and tribulations suffered by herself and her people, the Modocs, than any exorbitant compiling of literary finesse.

It came about in this way. My family had driven down the Sprague River behind a span of high spirited iron greys to visit this Indian family of the "old blood". After entering the plain, worn, unpainted house I naturally chose to sit beside the old grandma, for it seemed easier for the old and the young to find a common ground of conversation. My prime question wasn't long in coming out. "How old are you, Grandma?" I asked.

The room became strangely silent, as if expecting an answer of displeasure, but no, after long moments of deep meditation she began. Turning slightly, she said "Little boy, you wouldn't understand. Eighty-seven years are not many, but I have lived many life times in them. One was happy and free; the sun came and went over our lodges well supplied with meat; and Indians laughed.

Figs. 1, 2, 3 and 4. *Above, left*: **Fort Rock, Oregon, painted by Mrs. Moore from the author's description of the impressive mass.** *Right*: **One of the author's many colorful arrowhead collections.** *Below, left*: **Dry, cracked alkali bottoms. Eastern Oregon's ancient lakebeds seem desolate, but often yield priceless relics.** *Right*: **Mrs. Nellie Griffin bears typical Yurok tatoo on her chin. She is shown seated beside her husband, Seeley Griffin.**

"Then came dark days, when our women mourned for hunters and warriors that never came back. Men gathered around fires to make plans for revenge, and small war parties rode off in the dark. Children cried for more food, and campfires were fewer.

"Then, the Modoc people were driven from their homes on Lost River to this reservation. Here, on the home land of the Lalacas (Klamaths), we suffered much trouble. They (the Klamaths) wanted the Modocs to be killed, and even hauled off our wood for building houses.

"Then, Kientepoos (Captain Jack) with his warriors and families moved out one dark night for the Lava Beds; but again there was war, and the white soldiers were too many . . . ."

Suddenly her eyes grew vague, and as her thoughts drifted far away, there was not another word.

That fine old Indian woman had spoken some in English, some in her native tongue. The younger woman present filled us in with all the aged one had said. How difficult it is to place a value on this special source of unpolished facts; one who lived it. It remains a priceless gift from those troubled people who have now gone to claim their peace.

In this brief chapter, directed toward a better understanding of the Indian, this writer feels obliged to pay tribute to a grand old Shoshoni, Chief Washakie. By virtue of his versatile accomplishments he has been proclaimed by both historians and Agents of Governmental Indian Affairs "A fine American, statesman, scholar and fearless warrior"; a combination of virtues rarely found in any one man.

Washakie's wisdom, leadership and physical ability went unchallenged as Chief of the Shoshoni for some sixty years. His hard hitting, mounted warriors had successfully held back the Sioux, Cheyenne and Blackfoot tribes in their attempts to overrun western Montana and eastern Idaho. Fighting back these enemy plains tribes on his eastern flank could be construed as a strategic move to partially align his people with the United States military forces. It is also recorded that during the Indian wars of the seventies he rode in the lead of a powerful detachment of his own warriors, to maneuver General George Crook's army out of a situation threatening their possible annihilation.

Although on various battlefronts Washakie had volunteered the services of several hundred well-trained and fully-armed warriors, records show that our government extended no special terms of leniency in their orders confining the Shoshoni Indians to their small portion of this earth.

The disheartened old leader's spirit was badly bruised, but not broken. He would use his final weapon in defense of his people; a verbal challenge to his new government across the table of confusing papers and versatile words. His historical and final plea, given at a Wyoming Governor's conference in 1878, is recorded in a very fine, authentic book "Indians of the United States" by Dr. Clark Wissler.

I take great pleasure in introducing this outstanding writing of Dr. Wissler's to those unfamiliar with the masterpiece. He has given us the privilege of widening our knowledge of the tribal grievances brought out in Chief Washakie's "last stand" address.

We read, quoting Dr. Wissler, *"We are right glad, sir, that you have so bravely and kindly come among us. I shall, indeed, speak to you freely of the many wrongs we have suffered at the hands of the white man. They are things to be noted and remembered. But I cannot hope to express to you the half that is in our hearts. They are too full for words.*

"Disappointment; then deep sadness; then a grief inexpressible; then at times, a bitterness that makes us think of the rifle, the knife and the tomahawk, and kindles in our hearts the fires of desperation. That, sir, is the story of our experience; of our wretched lives.

"The white man, who possesses this whole vast country from sea to sea, who roams over it at pleasure and lives where he likes, cannot know the cramp we feel in this little spot; with the undying remembrance of the fact, which you know as well as we, that every foot of what you proudly call America, not very long ago belonged to the red man. The Great Spirit gave it to us. There was room enough for all his many tribes, and all were happy in their freedom. But the white man had, in ways we know not of, learned some things we had not learned; among them, how to make superior tools and terrible weapons, better for war than bows and arrows; and there seems no end to the hordes of men that followed them from other lands beyond the sea.

"And so, at last, our fathers were steadly driven out, or killed, and we, their sons, but sorry remnants of tribes once mighty, are cornered in little spots of the earth all ours of right — cornered like guilty prisoners and watched by men with guns who are more than anxious to kill us off.

"Nor is this all. The white man's government promised that if we, the Shoshones, would be content with the little patch allowed us, it would keep us well supplied with everything necessary to comfortable living, and would see that no white man should cross our borders for our game or for anything that is ours. But it has not kept its word! The white man kills our game, captures our furs, and sometimes feeds his herds upon our meadows. And your great and mighty government — oh, sir, I hesitate, for I cannot tell the half! It does not protect us in our rights. It leaves us without the promised seed, without tools for cultivating the land, without implements for harvesting our crops, without breeding animals better than ours, without the food we still lack; after all we can do, without the many comforts we cannot produce, without the schools we so much need for our children.

"I say again, the government does not keep its word! And so, after all we can get by cultivating the land, by hunting and fishing, we are sometimes nearly starved, and go half naked, as you see us!

"Knowing all this, do you wonder, sir, that we have fits of desperation and think to be avenged?"

So it came to pass that our swarthy Indian populous concealed revenge, hatred and surges of desperation behind tightened lips and wrinkled brows. The spirit of freedom smouldered for a time, flared up weakly at intervals, and then died out with the coming of the new generation.

Though the famous Indian Chieftains and Leaders of oppressed tribes gave their last physical and verbal strength, hoping to hold onto a portion of their hereditary birthrights, the white frontier conceded little. Unrelenting pressure continued through loophole paper distortions. These miserable, dark days of our Indian predecessors are not the ones we flaunt to the world as proud achievements of "white diplomacy", but nevertheless, the history is ours to accept.

I have conversed with several ancient Indian people who seemed to be living in two worlds; the accepted present, and theirs of a free past. They had borne the brunt of white domination since the 1820's. At times there were evidences of slight flares of anger, but in the main it was controlled beneath a blanket of thoughtful silence. The old embers had not entirely cooled. I marveled at the calm with which they suppressed the ache in their hearts.

The tendency to distrust most white men, and remembrances of losses suffered at his hand still exists in the blood of many tribal descendants of our day. A weather beaten old Klamath Indian friend of my family gave us an interesting example of this when he said *"Some things in the Indian's mind and blood never die, though they become weaker and more confused in a white man's world."*

His expressions in English were somewhat limited, but one accustomed to their laconic and somewhat disjointed deliverances could easily grasp the views he wished to convey. In his native way, and in hesitant English he stated that *"There are things within the Indian blood much like a river. The water, at the source is clear and pure. It runs along for a time undisturbed, and at peace with the pools that spawn the fishes. Then comes the time to flow on down between new banks, where other streams come in and mix the waters that become restless and form the river that often becomes muddy, and angry at its banks."* He finished by saying *"This is how I say some things are hidden, but never die in the Indian's veins."*

Well knowing how difficult it was for the old warrior to concede any measure of defeat, this brief narration came as a surprise. In substance the old fellow was saying, without jeopardizing his self-respect, that time had weakened his revengeful aspirations, even though the spark to do so lived somewhere in the waters of his past. This was all interpreted by the listeners as a sort of confession, with head held high by the principles of a proud heritage.

The inside understanding of these people who made history cannot be overestimated. I believe, were those old characters alive today they would appreciate very much the words we speak in their favor. I call to mind the many early day acquaintances who have said *"We are right glad you ask questions, and we are glad we have someone to hear."* However simple the words, they portrayed an eagerness to share their pent-up knowledge with an appreciative listener.

At the present time we are witnessing a most wonderful and amazing attempt by an aged Pacific Coast Tolowa Indian woman, Mrs. Amelia Brown, to pass down and preserve all possible of her tribe's culture. She is, in her twilight years of one hundred and four, with one day's schooling to her credit, instructing young Indian classes in the public school at Crescent City, California. Her greatest desire is to impart the knowledge she possesses of the Hupa, Yurok, Tolowith and branching, smaller tribes to the young descendants. She is teaching the fast diminishing coastal languages and tribal traditions, in an attempt to leave the young people clinging to the richness of their ancestry.

However, her facial seams deepen when asked of the days that white men killed their people and took their hereditary lands. Legends of the great Redwood Empire, crafts and spiritual observances have regrettably been cast aside by this steamroller modern era.

As our personal friend, knowing her to be alert, very likeable and possessing that bright, cheerful attitude toward life along with her great mental capacity, we are not so surprised by her late ambitions. The energies and accomplishments of this dear old Tolowa Indian may well be an eternal beacon for both Indian and White.

From this great contribution we anticipate a revival of the nearly lost language through Amelia's 25 or 30 young Indian students, for they are eager, enthused and quite familiar with tribal sound combinations. These, I find, can only be learned through verbal contact, and transposed into English while the old surviving members are yet with us. This is why we so appreciate the untiring efforts and gracious cooperation of these Yurok and Tolowa people.

To correctly pronounce their words or phrases as spoken, the hyphen is generously used in the Indian's talk, as well as in the English interpretation. Difficult sounds to master are those that overlap, fading out with a mouth and guttural combination or the sound effect derived from the unique tribal phonemic alphabet. For instance, names such as Da-gaists-seh, Yontocket, Taximith-dingh and many now extinct villages, among a multitude of similar tribal names roll off the Tolowa, Yurok or Hupa tongue with a musical ease that astonishes the renowned linguist. To further your interest in this fascinating tribal language, there follows a short list of words and terms taught to me by a fine old Yurok Indian, Seeley Griffin.

Poo-ook-wa-chel means dried deer meat; Nae-pooie, smoked salmon; Choo-oo-nappaw, goodbye my brother; Choo-oo-nay-way, goodbye my sister; Paa-ock, water; Poup-poupf, sand bread; E-e-e-eh, yes; I-ee-u-quih, a verbal salutation as howdy, or hello there; Nay-le, my eye; Chee-e-eh, money; Mus-koos-key-ah-saun, can't do anything about it; Na-taw-mare, friend; Nee-me-scoo-yan, sick Injin no good; Nau-ausk, papoose cradle; Shoo-ya-woogie, good white man; Sheh-nahts-meceht, rainbow more to Tolowa; Kawin, eel; Lu-mon, eel trap (derived from Klamath). This briefing has been rehearsed and used in conversation many times with my Indian friends, and according to them it is good.

The question often arises in the minds of the young "Why are the majority of Indians as we know them not using their native or tribal names?" I believe in reviewing our history we will find that this evolutionary changing was primarily due to the white man's influence; a natural thing that follows with the mingling of two different peoples and languages.

Indians were only known to the first white men by names in the native tongue of each tribe, a new language, words and people. As trail-blazers and scouts probed into the frontiers they were confronted by strange names such as Massasoit, Pocahontas, Pontiac, Tecumseh, Washakie, Sacajawea, Ekalaka and endless numbers of others in the native tongue. Scouts and traders were hard pressed for words to carry on conversations, and resorted to sign language, at which the old chief was a master in pipe council. He would go through an elaborate display of sign talk that only a few scouts could interpret, while tapping his own chest and repeating a tribal name difficult to pronounce.

However, in the closing 18th and first three-quarters of the 19th century, we see a widespread revision in Indian names as they heard and accepted more English. Though capable of speaking many English names they staunchly clung to their hereditary admiration for physical accomplishments, animal and bird life or all things of nature. From this period of Indian history we have become familiar with such names as Sitting Bull, Red Cloud, Catch-The-Bear, Two Moons, Red Fox, Thunder Cloud, Red Tomahawk, Gray Fox, Rain-In-The-Face, Bull Head, Blue Dog, Running Ghost, Spotted Tail, Gall, and Crow King. The list goes on and on. During this period and the one closely following there was another contributing factor in the abandonment of native names. Many of our frontier forefathers married Indian women, thus giving rise to numerous commonplace given and family names of the white people.

Again, in the early 1900s, we knew a number of Indians only by names applied to them by white friends and associates in a friendly, western spirit of identification. I have heard of and known several former tribal members as Modoc Pete, Tall Jim, Beaver John, Trader Joe, Smoky Jack, Pinto Pete, Whiskey John and so on. These names troubled me somewhat as a small boy, for I wanted to know them by a fitting name of the tribal wild. Why and when did these new Indian friends answer to names not theirs at birth or by choice? Then, I was relieved considerably by an explanation given me by the old fellow, Tall Jim.

He elaborated, "Mebbe like great warrior Kientepoos, all people say 'Captain Jack.' Many years ago cowmen ride by and say 'Howdy, Jim.' I go to fort and a man say to my friend, 'Who the tall Indian?' and my friend say 'That Tall Jim.' I go to store man say, 'Howdy, Tall Jim. What can I do for you?' Everybody seem to like Tall Jim. I like too, and maybe I be Tall Jim for all time."

This sincere explanation most likely applied to the origin of many such names among our fine old Indians. It seemed a most natural quirk in early western customs to address certain Indian characters by the easiest and most appropriate name that came to mind.

So, we gather that those circumstances peculiar to that period broke down the name barriers between the Indian and the White. As a united citizenry of today, we can seldom distinguish one from the other by name. Hopefully, this at least partially explains those questions often asked by the younger ones about bypassed tribal and pioneer customs on names to be and names that were.

A continued distrust of most white men was clearly evident among our Sprague River friends, especially the womenfolk. For example: *One of our Bloomingcamp buckaroos, Art Evans, asked a kindly old Indian lady to make him a pair of beaded buckskin gauntlet gloves. The price agreed on was $8.00. He gave her the $4.00 left from his last paycheck, with a promise to pay the balance sometime, soon. The deal seemed closed, so he rode off, and she went to work. A month later, when he came by to pick up his gloves, she handed him but one, saying, "You pay for one, you get one. You pay for other, you get other one." She got hold of her other $4.00, and went to work again.*

Nothing seemed to bring more pleasure to my boyhood days than to see some Indians coming along our way; either by horseback or in their old buckboards. It was there, on the front porch of the old ranch house that I really began to know our down river Indian neighbors; most of whom, in this instance were women dropping by to visit with Mother. There were those of a very serious disposition; some extremely shy; and many with wit and humor to spare. Then there was that loner, who sat apart and harbored a smouldering ill will toward another of different tribal blood.

This (generally concealed) attitude was accidentally flushed out one day when my mother went over to where a particular woman was sitting on the porch. She asked "Tiny" (so nicknamed for her one hundred and eighty pounds on foot) what blood she was. Well, with a dark scowl, "Tiny" indignantly burst out, "I got no blood! I'm Klamath." leaving us to confusedly interpret a proud heritage.

I once sat beside an aged tribal woman, in her reservation home, impatiently squirming and waiting for the right time to ask her age. Behind those facial seams were scars of confusion, suffering and sad disappointment. After long moments of dreaming in the past she said "Not sure. I live many years before we hear of a big war far away, where many white soldiers kill other white soldiers. I am tired, now. Heart heavy, like stone. Great Kemush understands."

No doubt this reference to a big war was pointing to the Civil War. Though sometimes taken too lightly, such live inserts come our way. In respect to those who would have it so, I feel obliged to commemorate the span of years I enjoyed these people as friends and neighbors by relating these incidents.

Only in these later years have I fully appreciated and realized the great contribution to our history those elderly Indians were leaving to our keeping, before crossing their last earthly horizon. It was nearly impossible for a youth, as well as most adults, to perceive the personal thoughts that lay behind those strongly resolute faces on which history had etched the suffering of wars, family massacres, tribal subjugation and the ever present white man's cunning; trickery, broken treaties, individual abuses, and on and on. "How, then," I have asked myself "could so much of the turmoil and individual persecution be so well concealed behind the features we had interpreted as gentle, sincere but jovial, trusting and relaxed in the presence of friends? Have we really mastered the word 'understanding'?" Fortunately, as the years passed I was able to at least partially read the thoughts behind those facial expressions, and gather much from their seemingly laconic phrases.

For instance, whole pages of early day inter-tribal conflict could be interpreted from a few words, as the following brief insertion shows.

This incident happened at the Gerber hay ranch, in 1902, near Bly, Oregon. It being customary for several Indian women to come up from the reservation to get the beef "trimmings" when butchering was done for the family and hay hands, several were on hand with their knives, bags, and of course, papooses in their swentz back carriers.

Though called "trimmings," there was some fine eating left to them; neck meat, shanks, tripe material, tail, head, heart, and etc.

All seemed to be going well, everyone trimming, washing and sacking, when suddenly, from back of the beef windlass we heard a woman's voice screaming shrilly. "You Modoc squaw, you take my paunch," she shouted "I fix you big plenty!" And a lot of good hair departed from the scalp that grew it.

Now this is meant as no reflection upon either of my good friends, who possibly made a mistake in dividing. It is related only to demonstrate how hard it was to control the old tribal ill-will under pressure. That one outburst, "You Modoc squaw" told the whole story. It had a tone of bitter insinuation. With my mother acting as peacemaker, all became calm again, while I, boylike, did so wish for a few more minutes of that fast action.

I hope these close observations of individual characteristics not only complete an acceptable narrative, but give the reader that warmth of human understanding of our native people. One good example comes to mind; a psychological blending of confidence, determination and humor expressed in a few fitting words.

Early one Sunday morning, on the Bloomingcamp stock spread near Bly, Oregon, Indian Pete (from down Shasta way) saddled his paint cayuse and called for his back pay.

My dad said to us, "There is something in the wind with old Pete, but I haven't figured it out, yet. Don't crowd him. He'll soon spill the beans."

Then we noticed his newly done hair braids, dangling from beneath an oversized, black Stetson. A bright red tie seemed to cast even more color to his already crimson face. Boot leggings decorated his pants.

He wheeled his paint around the corrals and bunk house, with spurs hooked deep, and shouted, "I go now. Catch me a maverick squaw woman! Got $30 in pocket. Shoot grub good. Want papoose, maybe nine! Feel plenty good. Crack heels like jackrabbit!"

With his mission that clearly stated, one could say he was ready to become a fam-

ily man. Old Pete galloped off toward the reservation, and was never seen by us again. I always wondered, though, how the nine papooses turned out.

Such were the simple, but sincere voices now stilled by time. As visitors pass through, viewing our extensive collection of Indian crafts and arts, I seem to hear an answering echo from each artifact.

From where I now stand, reviewing the successes of my life's work, I find the greatest personal satisfaction of my entire career came from an Indian lady who had come to see the Stone Age display.

She was amazed, and upon leaving said, "We Indians think it very fine of you to look for the work of our ancestors, and to protect it, as you have here. In time, our own young may come here and learn things possibly lost to them through the neglect of our own people."

This surprising appraisal by an Indian was the grand compensation I had hoped for over the years of gathering thousands of the red man's relics from his own sacred earth.

Therefore, in view of the foregoing glimpses I was given into the Indian's world, and acknowledging the personal debt of gratitude I owe to them, I say proudly "My Friend, the Indian."

Chapter II
DESERT HUNTING AND FINDS

CHAPTER II

DESERT HUNTING AND FINDS

The great central Oregon desert is truly the land where one looks the farthest to see the least. Yet, if one acknowledges its awesome beauty then that one has absorbed the spirit of open spaces.

It is rightly referred to as the land where the coyote's dismal wail breaks the stillness of night over your camp; where alkali dust sears the eyes by day and the jackrabbit's dainty morsel consists of greasewood stems and a nibble of ryegrass. The tricky mirage of nonexistent water leads on to more shifting sand. The horned toad scampers away and the white, cracked alkali beds are dotted with rustling sagebrush.

Your own legs must be the judge of how far you choose to walk out; and there still remains endless miles of "out," after you turn on the backtrail. This fascinating, wild land of silence seems to blot out the busy world you have left behind. Spellbound, you stand in the valleys of far away horizons.

Talons of the golden eagle and rattlesnake fangs remain as grand guardians of dim moccasin trails and lava cave dwellings. These lava rims and towering buttes once protruded above deep waters that lay cradled between mountains to the east and west. Our findings today show that untold thousands of stone points came to rest on the bottoms of these ancient seas.

From the remains of hundreds of old campsites, we visualize Indian life here as unbounded, untamed and unmarred. It is quite evident from the vast numbers of artifacts retrieved from this region the past seventy years, that the present sun scorched desert was once a verdant paradise for game, fish, and wild fowl.

Though cooling breezes no longer drift over ancient waters, and hot dust laden whirlwinds sweep the desert floor, I find it little short of wonderful to camp there. One can relax in the quietude of rambling spaces by day, and bed down under a blanket of brilliant stars by night. The air is often sharp just before morning, occasionally turning the camp white with frost.

Not only is this great region a retreat for Indian artifact collectors; many pleasant experiences await the recreationist who, for the first time, makes camp in these historic reaches. These people are fascinated by the ridge juniper, the aromatic sage, and the lonely, sturdy little bunchgrass. Words are inadequate to express the thrill of a desert sunset changing so suddenly to closed-in night; a peculiarity of this high elevation sage country. The scuttling horned toad may startle them; but he is harmless.

This chapter deals with areas in vast southern and central Oregon, east of the Cascade Range. Thousands of fine artifacts, described in the following pages, came from the area roughly boundaried by roads reaching from Lakeview to Burns, to Bend, to Klamath Falls, to Lakeview. These approximate lines are mainly for territorial references, and about as accurate as distances measured in "looks" by desert code; a term

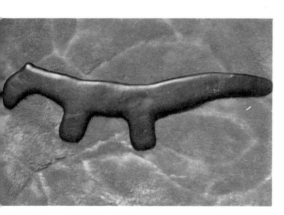

Figs. 5, 6, 7 and 8. *Below, left*: Unique hair fringed necklace, discovered by author while excavating in a Central Oregon cave. *Right*: Stone idol, found in Northwest Oregon. Evidently of Aztec origin, it was probably brought there by an early trade ship. It is foreign to all Oregon Indian cultures. *Below, left*: Slave Killer. Usually 10 to 16 inches long, and of dark slate. Found in scattered regions of the west, its use remains a mystery. *Right*: More of the author's beautiful collection of artifacts, taken from Pacific Shell Mounds.

typical of the desert pioneers.

As a young fellow, I rode the saddle over many of these spacious miles, walked as many more, traveled stagecoaches over and beyond, and "swamped" on freight outfits. With each experience came the opportunity to study this region's primeval volcanic disruptions. I could not refrain from mental ramblings, back into the past. How many early camps of the aborigine were destroyed or hurriedly abandoned as the earth opened, disgorging glowing streams of molten lava. What protection did they have from falling clouds of hot pumice? How could they escape the fires that followed? Did they beg of the Great Spirit to calm the madness of their earth? Yes, these, and endless other speculations were mine.

We have concrete evidence of horrible disasters that befell native tribesmen living near the snowcapped, twelve thousand foot high Mount Mazama at the time of its great eruption. Little did these people suspect the inferno brewing deep within that would spread holocaust for miles around. Geological science has placed the time of this volcanic eruption that formed Crater Lake at six thousand five hundred years ago. From these present desert areas, western horizons glowed with weird, brilliant clouds of pumice and gasses. Canyons became live rivers of seething destruction. Thousands of forest fires illuminated the bottoms of dust clouds carried by high winds over tribal habitations. It was only natural that complete terror gripped these primitive people, as the seventeen cubic mile base of old Mazama was blown from under her top; which, after a mile drop came to rest in her own crater.

We have ample, factual proof of human life being engulfed in various fiery, volcanic eruptions. A skull with its lower half embedded in porous lava has drawn much attention, while on display at local rock shows. It plainly shows that molten lava had entered the mouth cavity.

Another item of interest is Moccasin Rock, a footprint deeply imbedded in lava formation found along the old road between Paisley and Summer Lake, Oregon.

On the upper waters of the Rogue River, Oregon, a skeleton was found deep in a pumice hill. The sprawling position indicates the victim was probably doubled over, running, and was thrown forward by the impact; buried alive by its smothering tons. Alerted by these findings no doubt similar discoveries will follow.

Desert lakes are now little more than pothole remnants of the mighty waters once covering this area. As those inland seas receded to levels below the surrounding surfaces, the deeper depressions remained filled with water, leaving the present lakes. The water in some is clear and useable, while in others the alkali is too strongly present for humans or animals. Then, too, we see the alkali lakes fed by clear water streams, such as Abert Lake, where the Chewaucan (She-wah-can) River empties.

In time, all this land exposed to the scorching sun and hot winds was transformed into barren miles of sand and cracked alkali bottoms. Bunch grass, wild rye clumps, sage brush and junipers finally moved in on the great region, even as the loaded Indian travois moved with the receding waters.

Until recently few white men have challenged and conquered the desert's defiance. In the early 1900's, homesteaders came with great ambitions, energy and hopes. Soon, however, they left; even their patched clothing actually belonged to a man in a little shack that served as store, postoffice and "hitchrack" news center. A few men, with "never die" spirits and iron wills, such as my friends Rueb Long, the late Dick Schaub, and a half dozen others have for a lifetime outmatched the desert's odds. These men became a blending of silver sage, open spaces, whirlwind dust, summer and winter extremes, and big Stetson hats. It is an impossibility now, to even think of taking such great characters out of the desert, or the desert out of them.

Oregon's Great Basin is a most valuable source of historic, geological and archaeological information to those studying the existence and migrations of this region's man. Here, he can be traced from the periods of continental ice packs to the present shifting dust and sanddune wastes.

We find it difficult to visualize the sacred bond existing between those primitive tribesmen and their beloved mother earth. Special artifacts retrieved here indicate their reverence for nature's attempt toward sustenance from the arid desolation as we know it. Most likely, the Lakotas loved nature as no others and their words "Smile upon nature, and she will sag the smoke rack" probably rang true in this nomadic existence.

In my commentaries on desert artifacts and personal findings, the reader may note an occasional contradiction of conclusions previously stated as facts. For example: It has been said that nothing can be found on low ground (the old lake beds) except an occasional stray article that was dropped by some early settler or sheepherder. This has been repeated many times in good faith, according to their knowledge. Yet, I have retrieved thousands of points, stone figures and body ornaments from these same ancient lake beds. The constant scaling, cracking, water runoffs and wind cutting keeps bringing them to the surface.

The fourteen years eastern Oregon was my home furnished the background needed to do partial justice in writing of this absorbing, strangely fascinating and beautifully unpredictable land of the ancient ones.

Fossilized bone from the large, extinct animals lay here; remnants of the deep, dark, prehistoric periods preceding even the aborigine hunters.

With the Oregon desert's richness of archaeological material, even a first time visitor can find a tangible piece of history and take home with it a portion of the natural atmosphere.

From this single region has come the rare, abstract designs and stylings of age-old stone work now residing in my museum.

Fort Rock is one of the most picturesque landmarks in the Oregon desert country. It stands as a citadel in the gateway to a land of sage and sand, where tens of thousands of artifacts have been found in the last three-quarters of a century.

Geologists state that this unchanged, natural fort towered 800 feet above a glacial lake more than 10,000 years ago, and was inhabited around that same time.

Fig. 9 Fort Rock. For more than 9000 years this towering, silent sentinel has guarded the entrance to the land of sage and sand. Well named, its sheer walls comprise four-fifths of its circumference. Lake County, Oregon.

When volcanic action formed what is now East Lake and Paulina Lake to the north, some 2500 years before Mount Mazama's base was blown from under her top, Fort Rock was heaved up through the ice period lake.

Finds now show the existence of very early primitives in the Fort Rock caves and nearby butte caves. Dr. Cressman, anthropologist for the University of Oregon in 1938, pointed out that the sandals, basketry, bone tools and weapons found in a cave near Fort Rock were made by man more than 7,000 years before Christ. No skeleton of this early man has been found as yet, in that region, so we have no knowledge of his stature. Until the discovery of the Marmes man in Washington, Cow Cave, near Fort Rock was regarded as the oldest habitation of man in this western region.

After studying the superb works mentioned above, eyes are magnetically drawn to distant shore lines; visualizing primitive hunters as they stalked the now extinct elephant, camel, mastodon, bison and sheep.

We can be sure of one thing; no marauding animal could tear up peaceful camps on the massive, circular rim protruding high above and surrounded by glacial waters.

Quite likely, caverns at the base of Fort Rock, now deeply covered with shifting sand contain priceless basketry, sage bark sandals, tools and other implements of the aborigine that we may never see.

Black obsidian chips from arrowheads, knives, spearheads and other artifacts are here in abundance, scattered over the ancient campsites. Used metates, mano stones, pieces of pestles and other remains tell us of a once active camp of Indians. It was in such places they secured themselves against the extremes of summer heat and winter blizzards; or simply to watch the approach of hostile warriors from other tribes.

It pays to look closely in and around these old wind blowouts for lost arrowheads; and, if the site has not been re-covered by shifting sand, to go back over it year after year. I keep several in mind that I systematically check, and generally am rewarded with a few points. One is inclined to try screening in this exciting setting, but the area over one such site is usually 50 feet to 150 feet (or larger) and there is simply too much sand to warrant handling for the chance of finding a few points.

It is interesting to note the amount of broken pieces, especially skinning knives, that are found around one of these old sites. We assume that many fine specimens were broken in the process of making; also, that here in the main camp most of the skinning and cutting up of large game was done, increasing the chances of breakage. I have found many fine stone drills and punches barely surfacing, exposed by erosion in these well-established camps; so one must flip out every small piece showing above the surface to be sure of not passing up a fine specimen.

If the sand or alkali shows a man's tracks ahead of you, don't give up and leave the spot. Bend over and keep looking, for when the sun is low on the horizon you can often catch the glint of flaking, revealing treasures the party ahead failed to see.

The 23-inch pestle in Fig.10 is well made and of unusual length. It seems reasonable to assume that it was lost out of a canoe in some manner, when the area was lake region; the bottom of which was covered with deep, soft ooze. The pestle was standing nearly perpendicular in baked, cracked alkali with only an inch protruding above the surface.

Investigate every stone, however small, that seems to lie deeper than the surface. I have made a habit of kicking out any smooth or rounded stone in question, which has paid off in more than one fine relic. The same picture shows 2 short pestles, left; 2 oval mano stones; 2 crude, rough platters, (metate) well battered from much use; and 1 double knob hand grinder, which was also buried beneath the surface exposing only the dark end of one knob (Fig.10).

It is sound advice to look carefully around and through a clump of greasewood brush that has held the old dirt longer, as in Fig.10. This same clump gave up a fine 2-inch arrowhead, found only because I stopped to take this picture and repack my back load. Many specimens of arrowheads and an especially fine two-ringed, heavy pestle were found within 100 feet of here; close to the spot where the long one showed up.

Figs. 10, 11, 12 and 13. *Above, left:* The reward of two days of searching the trackless sand and alkali. The double knob grinder (right) and the 23 inch pestle are both rarely found items. **Right:** This group of grinding stones came from an Indian campsite covering an area of about one half an acre. The desert wind had "blown out" the site, exposing the stones. *Below, left:* Remains of an Indian campsite. Dark stone, obsidian chips and broken artifacts. *Right:* An average group of arrowheads, knives, spearheads, hide scrapers and drills taken from this vast desert area. Lake County, Or.

So, as you meander around through the raised clumps of desert greasewood, look very closely under low, overhanging branches that have matted down in the alkali crust.

Some may look upon Fig.14 blankly and with little interest, but it was taken to show some of the terrain where we found a number of our choicest Indian works. Many times have I camped in and around such wind gullied blowouts. I am on the trail at daybreak, to take advantage of the rising sun, the choice time of day for surface hunting on the beds of prehistoric glacial lakes. That sparkle on a flaked surface catches the eye; stopping you for a closer look.

Fig. 14 Wind cut desolation, typical of the Oregon Desert. The obsidian headband (Fig. 15) was found on a skull under the right bank. Lake County, Or.

Fig. 15 Obsidian headband. Such perfect ornaments are rarely found. Lake County, Or.

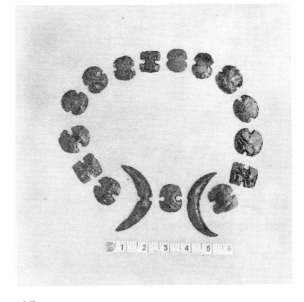

The Shovel Meal

It was midnight when I left my home on the Rogue River to reach the desert hunting grounds by sunrise. In the rush of packing, I had forgotten my box of cooking utensils; a disaster I discovered when I unpacked, ready for that long awaited breakfast. Now, this predicament left me bordering on despair as I am not one to smile when the campfire is ready, I have plenty of food, and nothing to cook it in.

Well, I wiped that mean, dejected look off the face my folks gave me, and began taking inventory of what I might possibly have on hand. "Not so bad!" says I, as the coffee was emptied into a paper bag. The can provided me with a coffee pot.

Most anything would suffice as a fry pan or griddle, but who carries a magic wand to produce the "anything"? I wasn't about to settle for less than half a dozen big brown hotcakes, smothered in eggs and bacon.

Ah! How about that old shovel? It was scoured and polished in sand. What a skillet this would be for the next three days!

A can of pork and beans was emptied into the small container I had hoped would hold arrowheads. This can made a splendid batter utensil.

My old shovel went over the fire. Now, this was all an experiment, but one success followed another. Fried bacon was first pushed up next to the handle; followed by fried eggs; which left plenty of shovel blade to brown that de- - licious hotcake.

Tableware was plentiful; a pocket knife, greasewood chopsticks, and a pair of pliers. My four-inch trowel served as both pancake turner and spoon. What more could one ask for?

So, with a gracious shovel meal consumed by daintily wielding a loaded plasterer's trowel, the early morning hunt went off on schedule. Many artifacts were found, and my stomach was pleasantly full.

Point Hunting

One plan, studied, tried and proven to be good in certain localities over this vast south-central Oregon desert country, has netted me several hundred arrowheads.

I had been crossing and recrossing a nearly mile-wide strip of an old lake bottom. Finally, I noticed that points were mostly being found in a certain line, almost crosswise to the course I was taking. In this cross section where fire cracked rock showed up at intervals, I began pulling up sagebrush, sticking them upside down in other bushes, to serve as markers. The following day I noticed the ¼ to ½ mile of bush markers formed a line continuing out from a higher point of land, on the old shore line.

It struck me, then, that as the vast area of ancient waters was receding, long, low, narrow peninsulas of sand began to protrude out into the remaining water body. Indian seasonal camps had followed out onto these low necks. Naturally, this would give them shorter water routes, and place them in the midst of water fowl flights. Where Indians established camps, one finds the telltale signs of cracked and broken campfire rocks.

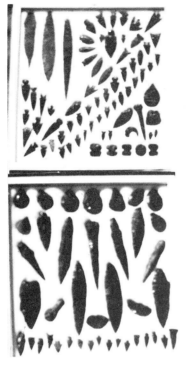

Figs. 16, 17, 18 and 19. *Above, left:* Found within a quarter mile radius, this wide range of styling shows an overlapping of tribes. *Right:* A fine lot of spearheads, points, punches and needle sharp knives from the Oregon Desert. *Below, left:* Lava mortar; 18 inches high, with a 15 inch diameter. Reassembled from seven scattered, buried fragments. Found by probing marsh sod with sharp steel rod. *Right:* A twenty pound rotation pestle, used for crushing. Especially good for seed grinding. Fig. 18, Klamath County. Others, Lake County, Or.

Centuries of wind and water action have removed the low sand strips, letting the broken rock and arrowheads come to rest on now dry lake bottoms. Thousands of arrowheads were made on these ancient necks, as the numerous small patches of obsidian chips prove.

Stake out the old line of hunting campsites, until the picture is pretty clear in your mind. Look closely parallel with, and out approximately 300 feet on both sides of the bush markers, for the lost arrowheads. Once you know where the original sand strips laid, no time should be lost.

Why there are such concentrations of arrowheads along these lines, we can only guess. Possibly, many points were lost from the volleys of arrows shot into flocks of wild fowl. Or, perhaps they were lost during target shooting at floating objects, etc. Whatever the conclusion, I have over 1000 fine points, obtained by following this unique plan.

The Three Year Mortar Search

I was down on the hunter's "firing line," south of Klamath Falls, Oregon, bordering the game refuge. There, a portion of one side of the large lava mortar shown in Figure 18 was found. Hours of turning over every rock in sight did not bring forth any more of the mortar.

The next year I went back, equipped with a long, pointed half-inch rod to probe the ground and tule beds, in hopes of locating the rest of my interesting mortar. Squares of 10 feet were staked out over the spot where I had found the first half-buried piece. I jabbed and probed every 2 to 3 inches in that square. Each time a rock was felt, it was not a part of my project. The tiring efforts finally paid off, when, 4 inches deep, the bottom and a large circle of the top was found.

The following year a third search was made, and the other four segments were found with the pointed bar. This completed the search, and after cementing it together, the mortar (weighing around 100 pounds) had a place in my collection.

This procedure might not work out in a hundred attempts. It was done strictly as an experiment, and just happened to beat the odds.

Although the surface has been well looked over in this strip of Indian habitation south of the "firing line," I am convinced that some fine artifacts are yet beneath the surface.

Mortars, Pestles and Gristmills

From a thorough study of mortars, I find it impossible to dovetail a certain type into a particular locality; the next find may completely reverse one's theory. The Klamaths, when first contacted by white men, were grinding "wocus" in flattened bottom mortars that sat upright on camp floors. To the north and east on sandy desert floors, metates and pointed or cone-shaped bowls were used. These tall, cone shapes were set in sand, to a depth of about one-third or one-half their height, which held them firmly. Also, in Fort Rock Valley I have found both flat bottomed and concave bottomed mortars. In the Klamath lakes region, we occasionally find some very fine cone-shaped ones. Again, around the Goose Lake region both distinct types have been found in the same habitation site, leaving us with something more to ponder upon.

So, one finds it debatable to say definitely that a particular type of mortar was made and used exclusively, in given bounds. We do know that the deep, cone-shaped ones are found mostly east of the Cascades, and the round, bowl type is typical of areas west of the summit. The old flat metate, or grinding board and mano stone seems to have been used all over the west, from times primeval to the Indian's conversion to modern utensils. We are certain of one thing, the famous stone grinding mortar represents more years of patient work and use in the Indian camp than any other artifact left behind.

"Wocus" was a staple food of Indians in the lake regions of Lake and Klamath counties. Seed from the yellow water lily was mortar ground into flour; from which a wholesome bread was baked, using hot rocks or hot sandpits. Inland Indians of the Pacific slopes were blessed with the acorns of the oak tree. They ground their bread flour from this. It first had to be processed in fresh water, to remove the bitter tannic acid. Yurok Indians called their bread "paup-saufp."

Sand Bread

By special invitation, my wife and I were once privileged to watch an elderly Indian woman demonstrate the art of making sand bread. She was eager and smiling, which made it easy to ask questions; complimentary gestures to a friend, seldom extended to a stranger.

Screened and washed gravel was heated around the fire, which was built inside an outer ring of large rock in an area about four feet in diameter. When the gravel next to the outer ring of rocks was just the right temperature, it was raked to one side and smoothed off. She poured the dough onto the hot sand, and with a driftwood stick raked hot rocks over the top. A wrinkled smile and an affirmative nod said the cooking time was up; whereupon she flipped out the golden brown pattie, tapped rocks off of its sides and said, "There, – a good one!"

We thank this likeable Indian lady, now past one hundred and four years old, for showing us in person the actual development of a nutritious food from raw acorn kernels.

Food grinding was extremely important in the native's mode of life. Roots, tubers, seeds, bulbs, dried berries or dried meats were all made more palatable this way. Mixed in a bowl to which water was added, it made a sort of gruel. Dropped onto a hot rock, they were cooked, and these dried particles softened to taste as they were being eaten.

Indian women have told us the papoose was often given a hunk of smoked eel, jerky, or dried fish to suck on; but it took a good helping from the old steaming mortar to put that little redskin at peace with the world.

41

Figs. 20, 21, 22 and 23. *Above, left:* Small portion of 1965 desert finds. Drills (upper right) and fish gigs (top, center) are specimen pieces. Many more await future hunters. Lake County, Or. *Right:* The food mortar represents patience and hard work to attain symmetry in its shape. No artifact represents a greater length of construction time. This 17 inch specimen gives us much to consider. Lake County, Or. *Below, left:* This acorn mill is in solid volcanic rock. The grinding holes are 18 inches around, up to 15 inches deep, and are cone shaped. Sutter County, Ca. *Right:* Many bedrock mortars such as this are in the hills near Oroville, Ca.

We might also consider the unfortunate ones who had lost their teeth. In several mouths, I have found molars missing, and jawbones healed over smooth and bare, showing an earlier removal. Two showed jawbone damage, possibly due to hammering, or prying out.

No doubt thousands of fine mortars are yet buried along river banks, marsh borders, lake shores, and close to old-established campsites. They will mainly be found with bottoms up, to assure against their filling with water, and breaking in a "freeze." So take a second look at that rounded stone in these locations; it could be a fine specimen just surfacing from erosion. Many tribes hid them in inconspicuous places back from camp, when leaving for seasonal hunting trips. Groups of five to ten or more, found in Lake and Klamath Counties, show this to be so. Why they failed to return and use the valuable mortars, we can only speculate.

Gristmill Sites

Though not from the Oregon Desert, Figures 22 and 23 may perhaps present something unique to the reader. These massive clusters of grinding holes are commonly called acorn gristmills. These are located in Butte and Sutter Counties, California. Dirt, rotted leaves and dry grass was cleaned off these, and other gigantic rock slabs, to get a good assortment of pictures. These unique gristmill sites were first discovered in the rolling hills out from Oroville, California. Then new, uncovered ones were located in various spots over the aforesaid counties. Hot summer is the time to look for these gristmill sites.

The symmetrical holes fill with dirt, and grass grows over the entire base slab. Then, the summer heat turns it yellow, like the surrounding hill grass. Here is the clue my son-in-law, Herb, and I work from. Where the ground-out holes are, the grass is just a shade greener and slightly taller, because they hold the rain water longer. This leaves a barely noticeable, spotted effect on the surface. It can be detected, if you're looking for it.

Our minds visualized the many Indian women sitting around those stationary gristmills; pounding and grinding acorns by the tons. An old-timer living at the Buttes told us that until the mid-1900's, groups of Indians came there from the coastal regions, to make flour for winter. He said bag after bag was filled, until their ponies (and many of the Indians, themselves) were loaded with packs for home. One thing for certain, no one was going to steal their grinding mortars, while they were away. I feel Figures 22 and 23 are rare and beautiful sights. Only one thing kept me from taking the 18-unit one home; the estimated weight of twenty-five to thirty-five tons.

The approximate northern half of California, from around Bakersfield to the vicinity of Weed, was held by many tribes. The Wintun, Yokut, Maidu, Miwok and other lesser tribes were all classified as Penutian speaking people.

The oak tree thrives well in poor soil, standing on arid flats and sweltering hillsides, alike. It withstands long periods of drought; yet has produced the greatest bread basket in the Penutian domain.

43

Fig. 24 Approximately one third of our collection of mortars, pestles, mano stones, metates and double handled grinders.

Sneaky Acorn Bread

As an experiment, I ground out a pail of acorn kernels with mortar and pestle, leaching out the tannic acid and other bitter elements with water. Fine, rich tasting biscuits and muffins were made from the flour. (There is a little sneaker, here; we did use a pinch of baking powder.) Our good Indian friend, Amelia Brown says, "Baking powder fine thing our mothers didn't have. Makes dough go poof!"

We marvel at the highly developed skill those Penutian people have shown in basket making. This super talent seemed to prevail in most known tribes. The northwest California Yurok (a mystery branch of the eastern Algonquin Family) is widely known for their exceptionally fine basketry. Nellie Griffin, now 106 years old, is regarded as one of the best. The Yuroks have retained their ancestral characteristics, and I find my friends very interesting people to converse with.

44

Figs. 25 and 26. *Left:* Shown are three main types of grinding implements; deep cone mortar with pestles; hollowed out metate with mano stones; boulder (bowl type) mortar with shorter pestle. *Right:* A special touch has been worked into each of these grinders from Klamath Lake, Or.

45

Fig. 27 This cluster of stationary mortars helps us evaluate the extensive use of acorn flour by the primitive Penutian people. Butte County, Ca.

Fig. 28 This type of gristmill is seldom found. It ran across a seven foot boulder. Sutter County, Ca.

46

Beating the Sun

Some days are real scorchers out there, one of which stirred up a bit of personal excitement. I had traveled through the previous night in order to be on the sunrise trail. A dazed road stare and red eyes mattered little, until late afternoon. That blazing sun offered no respite, and I was thinking "My kingdom for a little shade," when an idea drifted by.

I made the good mile back to the car; dug a trench large enough to lie down in, ran the car over it lengthwise for shade, and was down for a sorely needed nap.

Hours passed like minutes. Upon awakening, I was startled to discover that I had seemingly contracted a very heavy nosebleed. That wet, warm, sticky feeling ran from the corner of my mouth down, over my neck and shoulder. My hand went slowly over the area again, for a second confirmation. A quick glance at the fingers, and well, possibly you, too, would have welcomed the sight of a hand smeared with warm, dirty crankcase oil.

More Point Hunting

By noon the next day few arrowheads had been found along the sand ridges, so I moved further inland to search all known shallow water washes. These had been good in previous years, and seemed promising.

Patches, as seen in Figures 29 and 30 are seldom run onto, but are possible finds, around shallow depressions in alkali beds. Winter storms fill these sinks until water breaks over to slightly lower ground, washing off the surface sand or alkali crust. If arrowheads are buried beneath the surface, it will reveal them, as you see in these two pictures. The slightly lower levels may be unnoticed by many, in their intense searching for an arrowhead. After all, wind and water action here in the Oregon Desert is an artifact hunter's most helpful ally. If the fine Stone Age pieces lay forever embedded, even though very shallowly, your chances of recovering them would be many thousands to one. Such help from the elements encourages our hunting over good areas, year after year.

Hard surface conditions discouraged any screening ideas, although I did scratch around in these two great spots, with a knife blade; coming up with four more nice points. Arrowheads are set so firmly in the baked alkali crust, that if one were to dig out chunks to break through a screen most points would be damaged, anyway. We should leave them unblemished, and look to erosion for future archaeological discoveries. Personally, I gain a great deal of satisfaction when I see how well the workings of nature has provided such fine protection of the art.

Remember, when searching over old prehistoric lake areas to look out across the wastes: you can locate one-time lake shores by the color shades of greasewood and sagebrush. There is a difference. This fact has been proven to members of my family on occasion, by my simply pointing out a mile ahead where we would find slightly rising banks, encircling now dry beds. These are the important little details that contribute to the success of a lifetime collector of Stone Age Indian relics.

47

Figure 31 was taken in a sizzling "110 degrees and no shade " in a wind swept blow-out filled with quivering heat waves. Those who have hunted the desert in August well know what I mean. The picture represents much more than meets the eye, being a typical study lesson of arrowhead locations. Around the perimeter, where the wind was knifing away at that sanddune and at about floor level, I have made some good finds. Sage and greasewood holds the cutting sand longer, and also keep the points covered a little longer; out of sight from hunters. I have found up to two dozen perfect ones in some of these weathering away perimeters. There may be only a quarter of an inch showing, but they are there, so bend low and look closer. Thoughts of "Old Sol" are cast aside, as you sweat them out of the ground and tongue off the black beauties, before buttoning them in a shirt pocket. This cleaning process is the most natural thing to do. Show me a desert hunter who hasn't tasted alkali from a beautiful arrowhead.

Point Hunting Patterns

Later, I experimented with a new idea to locate more points on sage-dotted open areas. A drawing was made, representing a five-hundred yard square, with fifty dots placed roughly over it as arrowheads. Rambling lines were crossed and recrossed, back and forth, as my own tracks showed I had done the day before, missing many points. I then drew straight lines across the area, at one-hundred-foot intervals, (inverted sage-bush markers do, in actual field work) then drew zig-zag routes back and forth over the markers, not over fifty feet on either side. Most points would then be seen. Too many artifacts and time can be lost, meandering around over your own tracks all day. Two drawings closely follow, showing the proven test pattern used in old lake bed hunting. See Figs. 33 and 34.

Newberry Crater

The massive ledge of obsidian in Figure 32 was nature's gift to the Indian tribes of Oregon and surrounding territory. Some ninety percent of their knives, arrow points, ceremonial blades, spearheads and other artifacts were made from it. Here lay countless thousands of tons of volcanic glass that worked out beautifully. It perfectly filled the prehistoric and historic Indians needs of good stone.

The marker or plaque alongside this ledge reads, "First discovered by white man in November 1826, by Peter Ogden. This Newberry Crater was named for Dr. J. S. Newberry, physician and scientist with Pacific Railroad Survey Party of 1855. This caldera was formed when the top of a pleistocene volcano some 10,000 feet high collapsed, probably as a result of escaping lava from side rifts. Later, volcanic activity was renewed, lasting until a few centuries ago." Location; Paulina Lake, Oregon.

Throughout this western region we find obsidian from this massive site, and other similar deposits, had a wide distribution; showing the great value placed on it. Heavy chunks were carried as far as two hundred and fifty miles before the Indian knew of horses. Very few artifacts have been found at these sites, which reaffirms that most of the finish work was done at the home campsite. From the twelve- to sixteen-inch blades

Figs. 29, 30, 31 and 32. *Above, left:* This surprise find was photographed before author stepped onto it. A beautiful sight, indeed—14 fine artifacts lying untouched in a wash between two shallow sinks. *Right:* Second rare discovery, similar to Fig. 29. Artifacts lay like crop ready for harvesting. *Below, left:* Old Sol masters this day; beating down on scattered mano stones, pestles, arrowheads, "workshop" spawls and author. All, Lake County, Or. *Right:* Son-in-law, Herb Edwards, stands on massive rim of obsidian, nature's gift to ancient man in western lands. From it he fashioned implements of peace and war. Paulina Lake, Or.

Fig. 33
DRIFT HUNTING = LESS POINTS

Fig. 34
PATTERN HUNTING = MORE POINTS

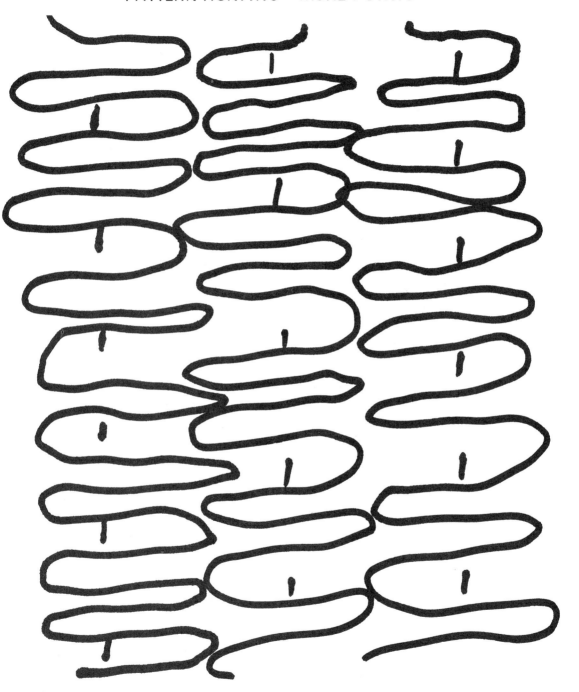

found, many miles from the source, we know the rough slabs taken home had to have
been very heavy.

Water, Water

*This three day trip south of the Newberry Crater came to a close for my son-in-law,
Herb and I, with only two more miles to camp. How we nursed those blistered feet
along! We were bringing in about a hundred nice points. The horned toads we were
carrying under our hats didn't have things so bad, though. Camp was broken none too
soon, for only one pan of water was left to do three jobs, —oh well, what difference if
dishes, face or feet went first, they all came off on the old towel the same shade.*

Abert Lake Find

*In May, 1960, the old camp car was again loaded for the land of sage, in northern
Lake County. Reports had been coming in that everything in the way of artifacts on the
surface had been picked up, from Lakeview to Bend, Oregon. This didn't sound good.
But I had a few places in the back of my head that organized groups of relic hunters
pass up, in their rush to get somewhere and back before nightfall. I had five gallons of
water along, plenty of good food, and a hankering for a handful of stars; so, come night,
come camp.*

*The first stop was on Abert Lake's east shoreline, where I had trapped for coyotes
and lynx some 50 years before. The old Indian Spirits had called for a heavy wind that
day, and all was in my favor. The wind sucked waves higher and higher, which washed
and moved sand, mud and gravel from the shore slopes. This was good. A few arrowheads were found up along the lake, but my interest had become centered on a batch
of lake weed, caught on something where the waves broke.*

*Between the barely submerged rocky reef (which it rested upon) and the shore,
was a mud strip about 12 feet across. As the waves ran out, I made a dive into it, to
reach the grass wad. Down I sank, into that blue-gray ooze to my knees. That was the
moment my shoes, socks, and pants came off. A most unique discovery was mine! The
object turned out to be the perfect red lava mortar, weighing about 90 pounds, shown
in Figure 35.*

*Now, to get that heavy boulder across the mud channel to solid ground! I could
pick it up, but the thing pushed me all the deeper into the sucking mud. Thirty minutes
of floundering netted me half the distance to solid ground. Then, I dropped the mortar,
which sank instantly out of sight.*

*The situation looked somewhat doubtful now, but it was also quite evident I
couldn't and wouldn't give up the specimen after having had it in my arms. One fact
was clear; it was now or never. After a long, steady lift the old relic was nearing surface.*

*Too late, I discovered that my feet refused to take the intended step forward.
The old caboose mashed down in about twenty inches of sucking lake ooze. With*

ninety pounds of submerged rock in my lap, those high waves rolling in didn't help the outlook for me, now bogged down as I was to the arm pits. The only way to move the bowl toward shore was to get it into my arms, and, with feet still bogged down, take a long breath and fall forward three or four feet. Of course the mortar sank beneath the water each time, but by repeating the falling forward tactics I finally rolled it out onto the shore.

Next came the job of scraping off a mud-plastered body (mine) in the high, hot wind. I then rolled, pushed and lifted the hard-earned trophy up through sand and sage-brush to the car. I might add, my skin wasn't quite as dry and drawn after streams of perspiration cut soft channels through the dry alkali mud plaster.

That night on Crooked Creek a big campfire licked out into the shadows, while I slipped into a clear water hole for that much needed wash down. Mosquitos swarmed in for their fill of a collector's blood. Just give a cloud of those boys a square inch of hide above water, and it's full of sieve holes the first pass.

There is one time belonging solely to the individual who has just finished a twelve-hour day in search of Stone Age artifacts. You crawl into a sleeping bag, run your mind over the findings and experiences of the day, and plan the next day. Somewhere along the line, you cease to make sense and daylight has again crept in over camp.

Sleeping Bag Companions

To continue this streak of good luck, I pulled up camp, to establish a new one in Fort Rock Valley, about 80 miles to the north.

A summer night camp in this sage land and far away hills is one to reflect upon. Silence grips the night, as one zips up the old sleeping bag and is tempted to reach up there for a handful of stars. The yapping of coyotes on their night hunt soon lulls one to sleep. Tired legs and stiff back belong to yesterday.

To be sure, an exception slips in at times. All was going well on this particular night, when I was awakened by a foreigner in the sleeping bag. The thing took a few passes up one shin, but a quick rake of the other foot over the vicinity seemed sufficient, and all was quiet again. A little later, when the willful stranger crawled from one knee to the other, I need not say that there was fast movement in the old sleeping bag. Again, I had drowsed off when persistent claws seemed to be trying to separate two of my toes. That was enough! Being too tired that night to be run out of my bed by anything short of a rattlesnake, my feet went into fast action. From a wet gob felt in one corner of the bag, I accepted the battle as being over. My morning inspection identified what appeared to be the remains of a large scorpion.

Figure 36 pictures one of few remaining epitaphs of discouragement, privation and hardships in the lives of homesteaders in Fort Rock Valley, Lake County, Oregon. Here it was in 1908 and 1909, that homesteaders flocked to the basin with team and plow,

Fig. 35 Left: red lava mortar, found on Abert Lake's wave washed shore. Right: Suspicious grass clump yielded the beautiful 90 lb. specimen. Lake County, Or.

Fig. 36 One of the few remaining shacks built by homesteaders in 1909. A sad, silent epitaph, caught in the clutches of desert wind, sand and alkali. Lake County, Or.

Fig. 37 Typical group retrieved from a sanddune "blowout," covering about ¼ acre. Not a dry lakebed find. Lake County, Or.

Fig. 38 Reward of one week's search over lake beds and desert sands from Abert Lake to Fort Rock. Background, ancient lake bed. (1960) Lake County, Or.

to eke out a living from sagebrush and sand. Fifty years later, only modern equipment and money could challenge the land effectively.

This lifeless desolation is pathetic to view. The cellar house, which was never filled, has collapsed. Even the 4 x 6 outhouse has vanished, leaving but a memory of the old Sears Roebuck catalogue that rested in a box behind the door.

These old ruins seem to have one more purpose in the passage of time. Many arrowheads have been found close to the old building heaps. The ground that was plowed, to comply with "proving up" requirements, has now blown away, leaving some fine work exposed. It is well to look over these blown out plowings, as one drifts by. In one such, I found a 7-inch spearhead, and 12 perfect arrowheads. In another, 28 nice points were found by noon.

Figure 40 shows a priceless find from the Fort Rock area, and no doubt the prehistoric primitive laid away many more 9000-year-old artifacts; yet concealed in crumbled caves, or beneath adjoining surfaces.

Airplanes and Bodies

One day in this belt, the sun was hotter 'n Hades, and I had crawled under a piled-up arch of sagebrush for a little shade. I then noticed a light plane circling my car, about two miles away. The circle became wider, until one round brought the pilot over the sand ridge I was on, and right overhead. I assume the pilot had spotted my legs, sticking out from under the shady brush arch, for he sideslipped over me a couple of times, only yards high. It dawned upon this sunscorched, desert camper that the pilot had spotted me. He was investigating the possibility of someone injured, sick or already a set table for the "Buzzard Brothers; the boys with the nasty beaks." Hastily crawling out, I waved "O.K." The pilot made a couple of wing dips, and all became quiet again, under the sagebrush stack.

Metate Caches

For a change in desert temperatures, I chose to make my next trip in cold, raw weather, to carry out an idea that had been brewing for some time. Digging would be more pleasant in icy wind than in sweltering sun for the particular thing I had in mind. Having read two previous accounts where artifacts had been found beneath old metates, (as shown in Figure 39) I was prepared to dig under every known one that lay partially or completely on the surface. Some would be broken, many eaten away by wind cutting, and there were sure to be those turned over or moved already by other relic hunters. At best, I would have but a slim chance of finding one undisturbed.

Between 5 A.M. and 2 P.M. thirteen holes had been dug under old grinding slabs, and this idea no longer seemed so brilliant. However, when the fourteenth one was turned over, it seemed a better prospect. About twelve inches deep the shovel clinked on stone; a noise I had strained to hear since early morning. Figure 40 shows the grand cache of fifty-five artifacts, laid out and photographed on the metate and alkali that

56

Fig. 39 Old metates such as these are worthy of investigations, as caches are sometimes beneath them. Weathered and rough, they once served a useful purpose in primitive living. Lake County, Or.

Fig. 40 Exciting cache: recessed spearheads, tomahawk, pointed club head, knives and fleshing tools were concealed by primitive hunter beneath large metate (foreground). Lake County, Or.

yielded them. For a moment it seemed questionable that this collector would survive the excitement. You know, no matter what our ages that old blood pressure still zooms with extreme pleasure when something that great unexpectedly pops up.

Spearheads and Stone Clubs

Top recessed, handthrown spearheads are distinctly unique to any I have found in all the years of exploratory works. The bow and arrow was possibly a weapon of the future when these were used. The recessed head is indicative of a shaft made specifically to insert into the stone head, and thrown by hand or atlatl into the animal. We may assume the shaft was grooved in the end, and up each side, possibly an inch or better; thus fitting securely into the head without wrappings.

The primitive hunter could then run in when the huge animal became weakened, and grab his spear shaft. If the head pulled off, it had served its purpose in opening up a bleeding passage. The hunter could then quickly fit another head onto the shaft. The primitive hunter possibly valued the shaft more than the head, as the shaft would require much more time to rough out and shape into a balanced throwing weapon. Many spearheads could be thrown into the large, prehistoric animal within a short time by this ingenious method. I am not saying this was the procedure at the big kill, but it is highly probable.

The five stone club heads indicate hand killing weapons, used when a man rushed in close to crush the skull of his victim. The shallow holes seen on one face hold the handles in place while being wrapped on; grooves appear across the sides for securing the handles. With the presence of the axe and hide fleshers, the whole cache leaned heavily toward being that of an aborigine hunter. There was no sign of a burial in connection with the cache.

Figure 41 is the assembled accumulation of four days hunting in the great desert basin, and from years of experience I call this a beautiful sight.

Little has been written about recessed heads, for they are very rare. To my knowledge, only a few have come from Arkansas, New Mexico and these pictured ones, from our Oregon Desert.

Another interesting feature of sanddune country is seen in the peculiar action of heavy winds that blast away, up and over the dune. The remaining pocket-eddies are often rich spots. Most people hunt the windswept slopes confronting the prevailing winds. Contrary to most, I find better hunting on the opposite, or leeward side of the ridge. The wind sweeps up and over the top, swirling and sucking out eddies ahead of the dune; sometimes over four feet deep. These pockets then enlarge, and finally become a good-sized blowout, where arrowheads are almost always found. I have found up to twenty-five in many of these sucked-out holes.

Freakish things sometimes happen. I had finished hunting one of these blowouts, finding a couple of points, when I saw a tremendous whirlwind meandering and circling my way. It was an unusual twister, carrying everything from sand and dust to sage

Fig. 41 A much prized four day find in the desert wilds. Notice how dry weather cracks these old lake beds.

Fig. 42 Klamath and Rogue River points, found in the same sanddune; not often the case. Top barbs, Rogue River. Side notched, Klamath.

Fig. 43 Three of twenty recessed spearheads found buried beneath metate in the Oregon Desert. The shaft could be yanked out, and another applied quickly for killing large animals. Lake County, Or.

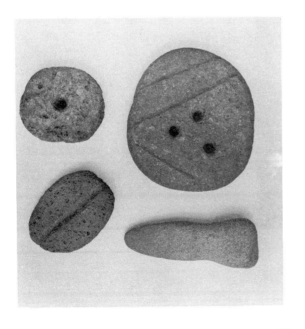

Fig. 44 Arrowshaft tools. Upper left, shaft straightener and sizer. Upper right, shaft rounder, 3 sizes of holes and sanding grooves. Lower left, sander. Lower right, splitting wedge. Lake County, Or.

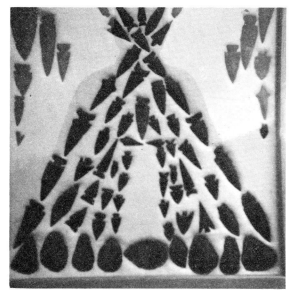
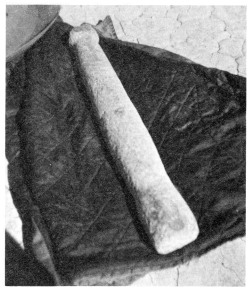

Figs. 45, 46, 47 and 48. *Above, left:* Arrowheads, spearheads and hide fleshers, surfaced by erosion. *Right:* This 23½ inch pestle was found in an ancient lake bed, below a cave entrance on the Chewaucan River. *Below, left:* Indian arrowhead workshop. Covering five acres, every foot of it is littered with obsidian spawls. *Right:* Author made his first trip here in 1905, picking up hundreds of broken spearheads and knives in the huge workshop. Apache tear breakage was immense. All, Lake County, Or.

branches. I ducked low behind a greasewood, as it tore past. When I stood back up, there, in the hole I had just searched lay a fine big spearhead, uncovered by that violent whirlwind. Quirk of nature or downright luck, I came away with a fine obsidian spearhead.

Stone Age Fishing

For substantial findings, we collectors are consistent in aligning Indian tribes with waters of some dimension. The primary thought in exploring for ancient sites is; "Where was their source of water?" It was the all important factor in establishing permanent camps. Springs, lakes, rivers, creeks, trapped seepage from rimrock fissures and bedrock rain traps are among the many we have to consider. The Oregon Desert is known for its many primitive sites as much as forty miles from present day water, which in itself establishes the time of habitation to a period of plentiful lake water.

Figure 49 shows a two to one enlargement of one of the ten stone fish hooks raked out of a crevice in a Lake County cave. Such relics are survivors of the deep water period, and were it not that most perishable materials have disintegrated long ago, we would most likely dig into remnants of old fish nets and seines. An old Indian friend explained this stone hook by saying, *"Not to throw out like you do with steel hook. Big fish swallow hook and chunk of meat. Then you follow him, and drag him to shallow water. Then finish big fellow off with spear or arrow."* So we judge this to be more of a hang on or towing hook.

Figure 50 is one of the five specimen fish spearheads picked up from a barren stretch of alkali crust remaining where one of those low, barren peninsulas of sand had one day fingered out into the lake. These previously explained strips of land, though void of any geographic outlines, have been my favorite hunting grounds since I first discovered how to use them. Evidently there have, in times remote, been heavy concentrations of hunters and fishermen camping on the long land projections; thus, the large quantity of game and fish points lost in the bottom ooze of lush swamp growth along shore lines.

Boat Anchors

The old stone boat anchors in Figure 51, although not artifacts of beauty, cause us to reflect upon dugout canoes riding the wind fomented whitecaps that once ringed the lush growth of a hunter's paradise. Thousands of arrows were lost in those vast waters; where, in time, shafts became detached from heads that came to rest in the soft bottom ooze. Stone anchors being heavier, they naturally sank deeper into the mud.

We can assume that more will be found as the elements cut deeper into the now dry, prehistoric lake beds. The ones pictured, plus nine others I have, were not found near existing mountain borders, but far out, where ancient waters spawned the white meated fish. They may have been lost when a rawhide line snapped, a dugout capsized, or even during a running battle between canoes. Whatever the cause, they are tangible evidence of another of the primitive's activities.

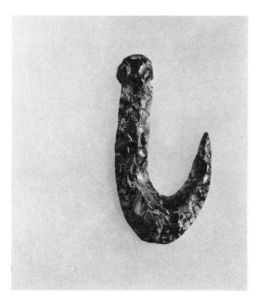 

Figs. 49, 50, 51 and 52. *Above, left:* Stone fish hooks hardly seem in keeping with today's barren desert floor. Remains of the ancient lake period, they were taken from a cave above the Chewaucan River. *Right:* This fish spearhead projects out into heavy barbs, angling away from the shaft. It is a beautiful and impressively efficient implement. *Below, left:* The stone fish hook, from 1 to 1½ inches long. An Indian once explained to this author that the fish was towed to shallow water to be "finished off," rather than landed as we do today with our steel hooks. *Right:* Stone canoe anchors are found today on dry, alkali bottoms and in sanddunes where waves once tossed above. All, Lake County, Or.

63

Burial Finds

It is my belief the 17 stone spike ornaments in Fig. 53 were once assembled with buckskin lacing and fringe to form a necklace. Each is beautifully flaked with an enlarged tie-in head for securing and must have been a prized possession, going to the grave with its owner. Curved stone relics are rarely found.

One very hot day, while shuffling along in ankle-deep sand on a ridge covered with greasewood the shattered, skeletal remains of an ancient one suddenly appeared, just under the crest. It was mixed with sand in about a three-foot diameter rough circle. The bone was much disintegrated, in fact must have been exposed for a long time, judging from slivered, crumbled, whitened fragments.

Many ask, "How do you know it isn't a white man's remains?" I have never seen an early Indian skeleton washed, blown or dug out that wasn't in the same sitting position; with legs crossed, doubled, knees close to abdomen, or with heels back under the hips. Whites simply don't bury theirs that way. Cheek bones are more prominent, and one simply "knows" by the wide range of evidence in the surroundings. Ofttimes the skeleton has settled to a side angle, or the body was first placed at an angle in burial; but never stretched out straight.

In this one the teeth were found within a rough circle of pointed ornaments, suggesting a neck piece. The stone pattern differs uniquely from any I have previously seen, leaving a field of speculation. Was it a design most pleasing to the individual, a medicine man's coveted regalia, or did it just materialize from competition?

It was at Fig.14 about two feet down from the surface of the right bank, I saw part of an embedded skull. It was facing into the bank, and as I carefully released it I found what was judged to be a unique burial headdress. Obsidian ornaments remained securely in the dirt; closely fitting around the frontal section of the skull, facing into the bank. This portion of the headgear consisted of a center disk, two crescents above the eye cavities, and seven rounded disks spaced equally toward the back, where the shattered bone had dropped away. More disks were dug out of the dirt below. This was a chance find, of course, and only because of wind cutting action was it ever exposed. The rare assembly of stone ornaments is shown in Fig 15. We assume that such a burial regalia was that of a medicine man or other member with tribal distinction. The rare group in Fig. 16 from the same sanddune offers a fine comparison of overlapping habitations in one small area. The rare 9½-inch dagger, third right, upper left, was the attraction here.

In all the years I have searched the big desert region, only four groups of body adornments have been personally discovered.

The valuable and exciting surprise find, shown in Figure 54, came one very hot day in the sanddune country. The picture was taken before the sand was tracked up, or anything molested. It lay at the bottom of a large wind blowout, alongside the high sand ridge. Wind had cut enough sand away to uncover the top portion of the skull, which I first took, from my position, to be an earthen jug, or bowl.

After a close study of the skeletal remains, both before and after digging out, I arrived at a partial conclusion to the question in my mind "Why were some bones whiter and more disintegrated than others, yet exposed here together in a mass group?"

It seemed evident that in previous years wind had made an undercut, exposing the bottom portion of the doubled up buried one, while the upper bones had remained imbedded in dirt. These lower bones had slacked, whitening in the desert sun until wind action again covered the entire skeleton. There are winds that cover, and winds that cut away. This time it seemed a blowout had started at the top, and quite recently, for the skull and top body bones still retained color, and were partially in place. The skull shell was too thin and fragile to carry in my back pack, so a deep hole was dug, where all remains were given another burial. There was a two-inch diameter charm stone, three ceremonial type arrowheads, (four to four and one-half inches long) and nine hunting points in this ancient burial.

I may, perhaps, be as close to the correct answer in my analysis of this find as anyone can be. However, factual evidence showed it to be a male, (identified by the artifacts in burial) and far beyond adolescence, for the teeth were worn off to the gum line.

Good Old Packsack

On a long day's hunt the packsack is filled with necessities for an emergency night's stay out. Occasionally, one is caught with too little daylight to locate camp, or becomes too fatigued to attempt the back trip in darkness; so, we just drop everything until morning. In the twelve- to fourteen-pound pack one finds a canteen of water, matches, a package of raisins, a box of toasted crackers, a tomato can and coffee. Not too much, but you will see another sunrise. It isn't bad, after one lies down alongside the sagebrush windbreak, to stick your feet in the good old packsack and watch that flickering brush fire in front.

Searching for artifacts over this entire western country teaches that singular patterns are to be considered in hunting each particular area. The expectation for certain relics is more pronounced in one camp or habitat than in another in the same general region. The arrowhead is the exception, being found in just about any area you name. The finding of one likely has little bearing on a nearby campsite, cache or burial. In mass numbers, however, they may be the key to a valuable discovery.

It has been my experience to find trinkets, ornaments, oddities, engravings and mortars closely associated with a well-established home camp; test holing and trenching usually turns up one or more old rock-encircled campfire pits. Should by chance the fire pits be discovered first, then keep an eye open for special pieces somewhere nearby. A few unique shapes, as seen in Figure 55, seem somewhat foreign to the Oregon Desert and are possibly so, for we see strong evidence of outside influences brought in by overrunning tribes.

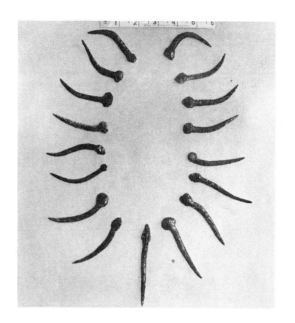

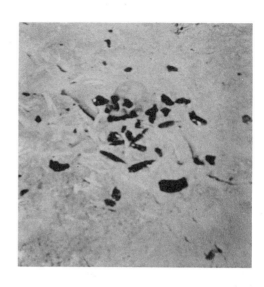

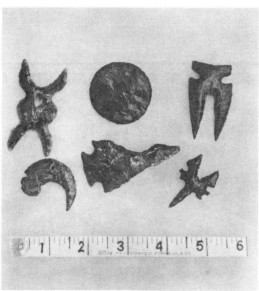

Figs. 53, 54, 55 and 56. *Above, left:* Curved obsidian spikes, believed to have once formed a necklace. This unusual group came from a burial find in a blown out sanddune. Right: Ancient burial, pictured just as the author found it. Cutting winds had exposed various portions of the skeleton at different times, making some of the bones more sun bleached than others. *Lower, left:* An occasional odd relic turns up around old, well-established Indian camps, such as the rare double pointed arrowhead, fairly common round disk, and fancy point. Also shown are a claw, duck effigy and unidentified specimen. All make interesting display pieces. *Right:* These fine, large relics are pictured side by side to help the amateur identify finds. Shown are two spearheads, one hand dagger, two knives and (bottom) ceremonial blade. All but Fig. 56 are from Lake County, Or.

From the early 1900's to around 1935 there seemed little reason to take much thought of who lived where and why; for arrowheads, spearheads, knives, hide scrapers and various pieces were picked up by the thousands. But the late surge of artifact hunters has taken its toll on the prehistoric beds, making it now compulsory to study the terrain in order to leave with an appreciable amount of relics. This is the explicit purpose of my book; to set forth the methods formed during experimental and exploratory work that required many years of personal study.

I have found no atlatl weights in the vast expanse of desert wastes but the recessed, hand-thrown spearheads. Three of the twenty found (Figure 43) appear to be a very primitive weaponhead. We believe heavy shafts were used with this type of head for a more penetrating thrust. The absence of atlatl weights does not disprove their being atlatl heads. With weights and thrower this quickly replaced head was probably the answer to the primitive's need of a dependable, fast bleeder to weaken a large beast for the kill.

The arrowshaft tools viewed in Figure 44 were an important part of the Indian's workshop. The wedge, lower right, is for splitting slabs of wood into smaller strips for shafts. The upper right shows a fine, complete rounding implement made from red lava. As the rough stick is turned and spun through the holes (three different sizes in this one) it comes out about as round as one can be made. The stick is then sanded and smoothed in the grooves seen across the face. Lower left is a sander, also. Top left is an arrowshaft straightener, or bender. With the shaft run through to the point of bend, or elbow, the stone is turned down to bring pressure upon the bend. It is then weighted down with a heavy rock. The time required to shape the shaft would naturally vary with the softness, greenness or grain of the wood.

The fine obsidian artifacts seen in Figure 56 were grouped and pictured for the benefit of those who are in doubt as to what relic they just found. Viewed side by side, they are quite different. Two left are spearheads, one center is a specimen hand dagger, two right are knives, and one bottom is a twelve-inch ceremonial blade from the Gold Hill site.

The stone saws in Figure 57 were most likely used in cutting off small limbs for arrowshafts and as a knife type hide flesher. The awls, or buckskin punches in Figure 58 are a few of over fifty in my collection. I have found these closely associated with old permanent campsites. The desert people of interior Oregon, and the Rogue River tribes from the Siskiyou Range to the Umpqua tribes of Douglas County, were highly skilled in the making of this long, pointed implement. It is known variously as a needle, punch, scriber or awl. Any or all are correct.

It is not surprising to find a wide range of cultures in the great expanse of Washington, Idaho and Oregon, wandering tribes having roamed over this territory from prior to eight thousand B.C., to the 19th century. Little is known of those people other than the fact they did exist, as shown by carbon testing of charcoal and bits of

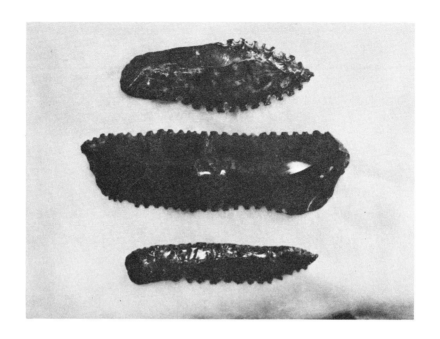

Fig. 57. Stone saws were used for arrowshaft cutting, and many other woodworking needs.

Fig. 58. A few of more than fifty awls found by the author in the Oregon Desert. They were used on buckskin and wood. Drills are similar, but have little or no head.

68

camp refuse. Our knowledge of the second or "Archaic" stage has been enlarged by the actual finding of materials and artifacts of Folsomoid bearing from caves; then above shore lines of the vast bodies of inland waters. Archaeologists have identified numerous findings as belonging to this stage, ranging from eight thousand B.C. to around one thousand B.C.

On display in our own collection are hundreds of artifacts associated with the second stage period. Folsom points convey the history of nomadic tribes and prehistoric animals in the verdant wake of melting icepacks.

While touching upon the Folsom Age I would like to recommend for your reading a 1968 "Special Publication of the Idaho State University Museum " Pocatello, Idaho. It is titled, "A Guide to Understanding Idaho Archaeology " by B. Robert Butler, Curator of Archaeology, I. S. U. Museum. The publication is a most generous compiling of educational findings on the evolution of western, prehistoric man and animal coexistence. I appreciate the kindness of Dr. Earl H. Swanson, Director Idaho State College Museum, for having sent me the Second (revised) Edition.

As far back as native human beings caressed the soil of this earth, called it sacred, lived by direction of the Great Spirit, talked with their Sun God and begged of the Holy Ground and primeval forests to grow their needs for survival, the aborigine was unknowingly establishing dates of his existence by the design, fluting and percussion grooves (or channels) left on his implements. The stone point and knife attracts us very much, and the finding of one brings the entire digging operation to a temporary halt for viewing, picture taking, writing up data, etc.

Although artifacts are becoming more scarce, relic hunters come from far and wide to pit their luck against the odds. Archaeological findings and documentations verify the Great Basin's contact with primitive tribes of the ice age periods down to the historic Klamath, Modoc and Snake people.

History has previously accounted the hereditary involvement, conflicts, border wars and uprisings from within the tribal ranks, which is supplementary to, but not in the same category as, this release on things to know about relic hunting operations. It is rather difficult to set the line of demarcation here, for one bears upon the other. For the purpose at hand, we have pointed directly to this vast region's phenomenal reservoir of Stone Age artifacts. I have learned much from experiences in these barren wastes and am quite serious in the things related in this chapter, especially my personal esteem and appreciation to those Klamath and Modoc friends who, as per previous references, had smilingly volunteered the knowledge I wanted, but did not have.

Desert Sunrise

Nothing in these wide open spaces leaves a deeper impression than the brilliant, phenomenal desert sunrise. I had camped one night in the western perimeter and at 3:30 A.M. the breakfast fire lapped up into the cool, gray dawn. There in the east, a picture was slowly forming into a living masterpiece that no painter, nor writer's pen could display the half of. At my feet, the first streaks of dawn had sprayed silver gray upon the sage, and hazy miles of sleeping desert to the eastward were measured only by the increasing density of purple hues. This blending enveloped distant mountains and rim formations, discernible only by their silhouettes against a crimson sky, now fading into the great blue yonder. Long, low stratus clouds drifted along, their bottoms absorbing crimson tints from the coming sun in contrast to their white, fleecy tops. I stood spellbound, gazing motionless at this colorful silence, how long, I do not know. The desert came to life with a blaze over the eastern horizon; the coffee pot boiled over; and a coyote's wailing cry rippled in from out there, somewhere. It was high time to apply the syrup to those pancakes and be on the trail of obsidian glints.

To an artifact collector such a morning greeting from the big country lends an extra boost to morale, and even seems to place a higher value on the day's findings. It is common for relic hunters to leave this great expanse of barren wonders with varying impressions of what they actually experienced, or saw. Even if they failed to name it, from their description we could still recognize the great western region famous for its primitive works, the Oregon Desert.

70

Chapter III
CAVES AND OVERHANGS

CHAPTER III

CAVES AND OVERHANGS

Needless to say, extra precaution must be exercised while hunting through, over, and into rimrock formations. It takes but one bad fall to break a leg, and one isn't going to drag that very far, alone. An important precaution to take, although I have never had to call upon it, is to leave a penciled arrow on paper in the car seat or camp bed, pointing toward the day's objective—just in case.

Rattlesnakes

Another factor to always bear in mind throughout the hot summer months is the possible presence of a lurking rattler. One false step down between lava rocks or over a shady crevice, can bring out that poised head, packing venom loaded fangs. On hot days, they will not be stretched out on top of the rocks where one can see them. They'll be taking advantage of cool places under ledges, boulders, in rodent holes, or possibly coiled around that bush you want so much to pull yourself up by. Take it slowly, to be sure, while climbing or descending over those rough, rocky faces, looking for caves, or while working one out.

Though indirectly connected with the actual finding of artifacts, the problem of rattlesnakes is bound to be confronted sometime along the way. If a few words of warning will spare one person pain, near hysteria or possible fatality, then my purpose in writing this has been fulfilled.

I have killed more than two hundred rattlers over the years, while gathering my Indian relic collection, and am in a fair position to discuss some things of importance to those unfamiliar with this poisonous snake. They are temperamental fellows who make unpredictable decisions. They may lie quite still, and let one pass close by; or run for cover as the one in Fig. 59 is doing, and then suddenly coil for a fight. Mr. Rattlesnake seems to know instinctively that this course of action throws his enemy off guard, in most instances. You may run onto one that has heard you coming and is already coiled on an open ledge, apparently afraid of nothing; striking out before you are even close. This fellow, rattling and striking with all fury, is easily heard and seen and can usually be killed with no difficulty. The one viewed in Fig. 59 is the dangerous rattlesnake that we all fear (or most assuredly should) in coming down from the upper rims, caves, overhangs, ledges and shelf rock formations. Stepping down over such places, where a person cannot see back under from the lower side, places all the odds in favor of the snake. Yet, people continually do this with little regard for the open target their legs present.

It is a mistake to believe the rattler must form a compact, strutting coil in order to strike. I have studied their capabilities of striking from all positions. The force is greater from a close coil, but I have pinned them by the tail and watched how quickly they can swing sideways. From long curves, flat on the ground, they can strike out at a foot with deadly aim.

Instructions to follow, in case of a bite, can be found on the inside of any snake bite kit. It is advisable to re-read them before going into a known rattlesnake region, especially if you are alone. Should you be bitten, and the kit is not along with suction cups, etc., a belt, or strips torn from clothing for a tourniquet and a good sharp knife will serve the purpose. Above all, attempt to control those fearful emotions and stop walking for a few hours. I have experienced this while alone in the wilds, and relate it only to possibly safeguard others from serious trouble.

Even with all caution and careful probing of possible danger spots someone, somewhere is going to be struck. Only one alternative is left to the victim. That venom must be bled out or drawn out with suction cups placed over the cross incisions.

Rattlesnakes usually crawl in pairs. When one is seen or killed move slowly, with an eye open for the mate that lurks not far away.

Perhaps after reading these few paragraphs on the habits and dangerous, instinctive strategy of the rattlesnake and a close study of actual pictures, many who have yet to see one may be more alert to that strange rattling buzz and avoid a painful ordeal.

However, the possibility of encountering a rattler should in no way dampen your enthusiasm. Plan yourself a fine outing into the high country of bluffs and precipitous rims. The better equipped you are to cope with emergencies, the more pleasant the trip. Long years of hunting artifacts have taught that "You can't have smoked salmon without getting some smoke in your eyes." A thought applicable to relic hunters in rocky, rough going.

The cave, or overhang shelter may not be open and easy to locate. Winds of the ages keep blowing up more sand and dust against the original faces, depositing a little at a time until entire entrances are covered. You may find just a crevice or small jagged hole at the ground line, or see signs of where coyote and lynx are using a run, back under the rock face. All of these clues could lead you to a good cave farther in.

Many ask "How are you sure if a cave is in there, or worth the work of digging out, in the first place?" Experience leaves us with but one answer. After a few hot, rough days on the business end of a pick and shovel you will either be completely disgusted and packing for home, or quite sure of a find and digging faster than a badger on a hot scent.

Caves formed of volcanic lava, in this high altitude, are quite waterproof. The preservation of perishable material can be excellent. Many fine works of art, yet unfound, will keep indefinitely, but are sure to be very brittle and difficult to remove.

I would like to stress an important piece of advice to the amateur, here. "If you cannot remove it intact, easily, then don't try. Find someone who can." A shattered mess that was formerly a prized, primitive work of art is as worthless as the midden from which it came.

I have worked out a system that has proven very satisfactory in holding together these fragile materials. It is described in detail later in this chapter. However, everyone to their own method as long as the precious work is saved.

Don't dig out old ash pits in some of these caves without protective breathing gear. The ashes and dust can be up to six foot deep, and by all means a respirator should then be worn. Through my own neglect I have come out at night barely able to swallow, and totally unable to speak a word.

So, keep in mind two very important things in central Oregon cave work. (1) Be sure to prod for rattlesnakes and (2) have that respirator in the pack. There is little circulation inside, and I believe no dust is quite as penetrating as cave dust. Work slowly, for streams of perspiration gather more ash dust; the very thing you should avoid.

For two days after climbing up the steep, rocky, rattlesnake infested cliffside I dug into the cave pictured in Fig. 60. It soon became obvious that someone had previously shoveled through it. This situation is not always hopeless, as my findings verified. Many times we find where amateurs, through no fault of their own, have dug holes, picking all over the place, ruining fragile relics as they dug. Apparently this was the case here; for pieces of basketry, matting, and fragments of arrow shafts were found in the center heap of rock, dirt, dust and bat guano. If a cave looks promising, then by all means work at it slowly and in the right manner. I choose to first dig down to the floor bottom, along one side wall. This provides an under face to gouge away from the bottom. Let waste fall down. Shoveling and picking from the top is a mistake bound to ruin any fragile relic. It is well to keep the area cleaned up as one goes along, so different layers of habitation can be detected and made note of.

If any disintegrating material is found, work a fabricated stick frame under it. The sharpened sticks should be taped together at one end, resembling a close tined pitchfork. This self-devised contraption holds the piece up while you work dirt out from the underside, between the tines. (Note Fig. 61.) A few coats of plastic spray hardens the material, sealing it against air slacking, and leaves no gloss. Acrylic Clear, numbers 1-10 is very good.

However, nothing of this nature was found intact; but under a previously overlooked shelflike floor projection I crawled into a nest of nearly one hundred obsidian points. This was a sight to behold or rather, something to feel, for I was on my stomach, scratching them out with my fingers. The existence of such pocket finds should encourage future hunters to go over "worked" caves a second time.

While working in these gloomy ceiling smoked shelters of many ages past, one involuntarily lapses back to the Indian's time of unmolested freedom. The surroundings prompt questions that find no immediate answers. "How many moccasined feet, large and small, have shuffled in and out of that entrance as freely as the eagle wings? How many Indian mothers have stood in the cave's picture window, watching their men climb from below with rabbits, deer, elk or wild geese? How many whimpers from newborn papooses might we have heard from within the folds of tule matting at the rear?" We picture winter blizzards swirling over the cliff face above, while dark eyes watched the

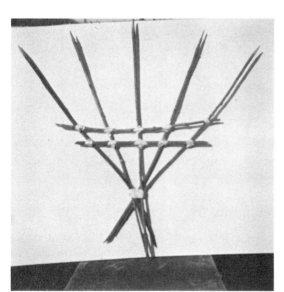

Figs. 59, 60, 61 and 62. *Above, left:* Most dreaded rattler is the fellow who lurks under the ledge you may be descending. Unable to spot them from above, legs make a perfect striking target. Jackson County, Or. *Right:* Looking out through a cave's "picture window," the desert is a panorama of shimmering beauty. Lake County, Or. *Below, left:* Fork-like frame, constructed "on the job" with tape and greasewood stems proved very efficient in the removal of fragile relics from caves, ledges and crevices. Earl Moore. Right: Shown is author's original fork-like "contraption," with tines pushed in beneath arrows, to hold the relics up while cleaning out from underneath.

deepening snow in the valley below through a flap in the protective skin front. Now, the strings of smoked meat and bags of wokas flour are replaced by bat and packrat accumulation.

Eventually, there came to those Indian people an ill wind that stank of black powder and bore lead spat from long, loud sticks. Lewis and Clark had discovered a route over the Rockies and started Indian talk to the north. Northwest Fur Company had their eyes upon the Indian's otter and beaver. There was Fremont in 1842, feeling his way down through the Oregon Territory. The Indians frowned even deeper upon cavalry and ox team inroads. Killings increased, and retaliation raids spread to isolated white settlements. The white military drove deeper into tribal lands and the Indian's revenge spurred them into losing battles. Smoke signals belched from lava buttes to lake shore tepees, but their numbers were weak and they slowly lost ground. They were forced to abandon cave shelters, to consolidate into more formidable resistance bands. So, moccasin trails leading out and down from long used caves grew dim, grass covered, and finally ceased to be.

Hair Necklace Find

One happens onto some puzzling finds hidden in caves. Always, you are led to wonder "Who cached this, and when?" The concealment of the necklace shown in Fig. 63 is of just such a nature. The lava walls and ceiling appeared to be of one solid, unfractured formation when I first examined it; but under a light there were indications of a strata some six inches high by approximately five feet long, just beneath the ceiling. There was also a slightly darker shade to the jagged wall surface.

Enough rock was packed and piled up to reach that suspicious looking streak, which proved to be a row of stones nicely fitted into a crevice. I reached overhead to try one for looseness and it came out. After slipping off the pile of rocks a few times, (strictly because of my own excitement) working my hand back into the dust filled recess, I touched something resembling the coarse hair on an animal. You may be sure I all but threw a perfectly good right hand out onto the desert floor. Another quick poke was made and nothing happened. Still confused a bit, I decided upon one more speedy grab to get a pinch of fur or hair so I could at least classify the rascal. It was a pleasant surprise to see a handful of harmless, soft bark fibre come out.

As the volume of dust settled I again reached in, feeling what seemed to be brittle buckskin and sharp points, embedded in more fine bark shreds, similar to the underbark of a tree. The large quantity was possibly stored for future construction of sandals, rope or matting. The removal of this fragile relic required most of the day. Overhead work is tedious and difficult. Broken segments had to be reassembled as they came out. I laced my shirt to a twig frame, secured the necklace to this, and was ready to leave.

Sudden darkness brought a halt to any further exploration at this time. Besides, I was due back in Rogue River Valley for a 7:00 a.m. work shift the next morning. Rocks were replaced, alkali dust thrown over the interior, and any traces of recent activities

Fig. 63. Necklace with stone claws, wristlets and hair braid ornaments. Some fringe work disintegrated, but as a whole it held together very well. Lake County, Or.

Fig. 64. The elaborate fringing, braided wrist band and carving on the handle strongly suggests this is a war club. It was packed in fine bark and hidden in a dry crevice at the rear of cave. Lake County, Or.

were destroyed, in the hopes of finding things unmolested when I returned. Due to reversed circumstances, this turned out to be the following year. I went much better prepared this time to finish cleaning out the old, deep crevice. A one pole Indian ladder, about eight feet long, flashlight, fork frame and cleanout rods were the main necessities. I was fortunate indeed, for no one had turned over even a stone in my absence.

Not more than twelve inches farther back in the dust and bark fibre lay another fine neckpiece, bone punches and the tule matting implements shown in Fig. 56. Manipulating sticks in the removal of material such as this is similar to your first go around with a pair of chopsticks in a bowl of noodles.

I would judge this hideaway cache of valuable possessions to have been placed there during the early 1800's. It seems reasonable to assume that after being disturbed, and driven out of home territory by white men Indians hid many of their treasures, thinking they would one day come back to them.

The war club (Fig. 64) was in a small, crawl-in hole. Many rocks were dragged out before I could go in on my hands and knees. Work was both tedious and tense, for one had to listen for rattlesnakes and inspect every crack. Back in some twenty feet, I was lying on my side, pawing dust from a shelflike projection when I felt the handled relic. When the war club slid out, the cluster of artifacts in Fig. 66 came slipping down in a fog of choking dust.

Quiver and Arrows Find

The quiver and arrows in Fig. 67 were found in approximately the same manner as the neck pieces. I had been searching for a shallow entrance to a cave where, as a boy, I had trapped. The location seemed natural, but in forty years things had changed. The entrance was now filled with drifting sand and dust. Late in the afternoon I ran onto a coyote den hole that appeared to be about where the old flat entrance should be. This hole was enlarged to admit me, going on hands and knees. At the rim face it opened up into the old, familiar cave. I assume coyotes or lynx had used the place for whelping ever since my last visit. I was ready then, as always, to fly with the first rattle of a snake and had come prepared. A fine thing, too, for just inside one was putting up a terrible fuss.

The bag of sulphur brought along was poured over a pile of papers and dry brush, set afire, and the hole abandoned until the next day. The sulphur fumigation seemed to do the trick, for I saw nothing alive in there while I worked the next two days. But just outside, beneath some lava outcroppings, I could start trouble with a noisy old rattler anytime during my stay there. I couldn't get at the thing to kill it, so at intervals went out to check on its whereabouts. After all, there was no guarantee that it wouldn't crawl back in where I was working and throw a couple of fangs into my hip pocket.

No bow was found with the arrows, which left me somewhat showing sad disappointment. The shafts are 32 to 33 inches long; 3/8 and 7/16 inch diameter at the head wrapping; 1/2 and 9/16 inch diameter at the feather base; tapering quite gradually from

Fig. 65. Cave caches containing items such as these matting tools, bone awls and necklace are usually in wall or ceiling crevices. Lake County, Or.

Fig. 66. These stone fish hooks, special points, thin knives and ornaments showered out of another crevice in the same cave as the necklaces and war club. Lake County, Or.

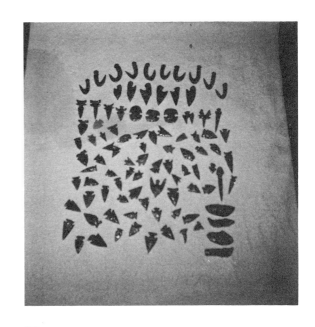

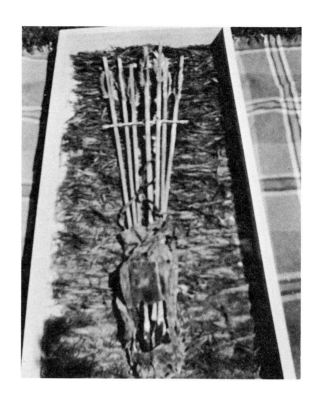

Fig. 67. Ancient quiver and eight arrows with heads and feathers intact. Hole has been cut in quiver to show the points, and stick threaded between the shafts to protect the feathers. They are sprayed and sealed to prevent further disintegration. Lake County, Or.

Fig. 68. Under massive cliff formations, we find Indian cave homes not visible from the valleys below. Lake County, Or.

end to end. These long, sturdy shafts fairly well answer a question I've pondered over for many years; why the big percentage of Oregon Desert points were made so long, narrow and thick? A well balanced arrow was the result, mounted on such stout shafts.

The lowly wooden digging stick is one of the most passed up and unattractive of all prehistoric artifacts. Yet, it is an original tool that has been developed into untold thousands of stone, bone and shell hoes, spades, chisels, handled picks, mattocks or anything the mind might conceive as an implement to move dirt. This tool of archaic lineage is simply a stick of convenient length, either sharpened or flattened on one end. Most go unnoticed, even by collectors and archaeologists. They are thrown out with the cave debris, and seldom does anyone credit the little sharpened stick with being the blueprint from which percussion, ground, chipped and pecked stone blades have developed.

Climatic conditions peculiar to a given region is the controlling factor in the preservation of perishable materials. High, dry atmosphere and watertight volcanic formations work as copartners to this end. It is amazing how buckskin, wood, grass or bark matting, sandals and basketry lay there beneath a dust covering for 9000 years or more, yet retain sufficient form and consistency to be carefully removed for display. Bark and plant fibre sandals, as seen in Fig. 69, are a much prized relic in inland Oregon caves and overhangs. Occasionally, segments or a whole pair are found. Bark fibre is found in sizable quantities, packed around and over such cached away items. Therefore, should any of this material come stringing out with the choking dust from a deep recess, you had better feel your way on back very slowly. This preliminary disclosure of a rare find has been my experience several times, and the thrills and excitement increase with each new discovery. These much used strands were stripped from sage, juniper and cedar bark.

Beneath the sheer rims that catch musical echoes lifting from the downward rush of the Clearwater River, (a tributary of the North Umpqua River) my family and I explored two caves, in August of 1958.

The deeper cave was well gone over, foot by foot, with the aid of portable battery lights to a depth of 250 feet, where a crevice was found too narrow to work a body through in safety. I am well convinced there are no Indian relics in this damp, silt covered, under-mountain passage. A cool draft drifts toward the entrance as shown by movement of smoke from a fired roll of paper set in the back. Indians simply wouldn't set up living quarters under conditions as summed up here. It was an interesting adventure for my entire family in this spooky, bat infested, dark passage; crawling at times, sliding on our stomachs in narrow crevices at times, or standing erect in dark rooms. All the while thousands of bats, disturbed from clusters as large as a wash tub, were snapping teeth, diving under ear lobes and parting one's hair that was already raised, somewhat. Then, as the light from our party farthest back dimmed into nothingness around a bend, nerves weren't soothed any when our little grandson, Doug, broke out with a scream that sounded like a cougar cry mingled with an Indian scalping party. But, this was cave hunting, and a four-inch obsidian spawl found near the entrance gave the clue to a real find in another hole about 15 or 20 feet to one side in the cliff face.

Fig. 69. Bark sandals, estimated to be nearly 10,000 years old. They were found by the late Dick Schaub in Fort Rock Valley. These were the forerunners to the discoveries made in Cow Cave by Dr. L. S. Cressman, University of Oregon. Lake County, Or.

Fig. 70. Caverns with smoked ceilings invite collectors to re-explore for artifacts overlooked during the earlier rush for baskets, moccasins, etc. Lake County, Or.

Fig. 71 shows the brush covered entrance to this approximately 10′ x 10′ x 18′ deep cave, that gave up the work of long ago. One must look closely to see some of these caves, as brush and trees have grown up over the years, especially if you are looking upward.

This dry hole, some six feet up to the base, appeared to be a typical shelter or hideout for a hunting party; also, an ideal lookout point to spot an enemy on the trail below.

After four hours of digging out rock and huge piles of wood rat stick abodes, I came upon a rock ringed campfire pit about six inches deep with ash, charcoal and small bones. Needless to say, spirits were running high by now and a test was made of all wall rock for looseness, or suspicious looking placement. A large flat rock was removed from a 2 foot diameter hole squarely in the back, where once again I had to remove wood rat stick accumulation to a depth of some 5 feet. This had to be done from a prone position, pushing or working rat material out alongside.

It was in this dry, inner hole that the reward came shown in Fig. 72. From an overhead crevice about one-half inch in size, I worked out the top part of an old skin pouch. The bottom section had either rotted or been eaten away, possibly by rats. Right below, in a 6 inch deep crevice, I found the nest of 68 nicely made black obsidian arrowheads. It looked as if they had originally been in the pouch above and dropped as the bottom gave way. Punches and roasting (or digging) sticks were in the back, along with 6 small stone skinning knives which were overlooked when the picture was taken.

Aside from the prized artifacts, this find means much in that it revives the ambition to search farther into this wild region of deep canyons and precipitous walls, where only deer and predatory animals keep open the moccasin trails once etched in the escarpment of the Umpqua's millenniums.

This rugged region shows good signs of caves yet unexplored, where future hunters may pioneer new finds.

Butte Creek Overhang

In 1961, digging was begun in an old cave overhang on Little Butte Creek, Jackson County, Oregon. Figs. 73 to 84 inclusive, show this rimrock setting, and the rare artifacts that came from it.

This site was one that required some study and test holing to locate the original floors. I felt confident that Indian tribes had occupied this cave sometime in the past centuries. To verify that a "filling in" had taken place, a bag of shale and dirt was removed and carried to the rim top for comparison. They were identical. Experimental holes then verified a three foot buildup in the middle, deepening to six feet at the ends. Previous water runoffs had brought this down, around both ends of the overhang, where filling and overlapping could easily be seen.

Next, we located the main firepit. A spot some ten feet out from the cliff face and under a projection of the massive overhang, seemed a feasible location. Beneath the

Fig. 71. This 18 foot cave was almost concealed by brushy growth. When cleaned out, it yielded the fine display shown below. Douglas County, Or.

Fig. 72. Arrowheads, digging or roasting sticks, and a section of a once laced rawhide bag, taken from cave shown above. Douglas County, Or.

smoked ceiling, one could envision Indians tramping around, eating and chipping stone; living a natural life, with the firepit in front and a warm wall to their backs. So, working upon these assumptions, a cut was made from the outer bank, horizontal to the rim face, following the original black dirt floor at about a four foot depth. The anticipated large pit was there, about half way to the wall. Heavy rocks ringed a deep ashpit, and things were now shaping up for a find. It is necessary to locate these main cookpits, for they centralize the foot traffic around the living quarters where artifacts are least apt to be.

Each positive development points directly to the possible concealment of relics. In this case, attention was focused on the back wall, a little deeper, following the graduated under contour.

Tracing relics is similar to putting a crossword puzzle together. The more blocks in place, the less difficult to find the last one.

Lengthy descriptions of excavations will be curtailed as much as possible; however, the findings, and ten days on the pick and shovel I feel rate many pages.

Twenty-five black obsidian arrowheads, a knife and a punch constituted the second day's find, all near surface. The work was more to the Rogue River Tribes' styling, yet made from inland Oregon obsidian. It appears that this much valued stone had caught on with this last, top habitation; a conclusion supported by the absence of points constructed from jasper or agate, the prevailing local stone. It is unusual to find a campsite floor with points of local design made from stone elsewhere. Evidently, they were a later Rogue conception of beauty and efficiency.

The next three feet down disclosed a second habitation, where points were of typical Rogue River styling and constructed of local agate and jasper. This ran true to form, and was accepted as such. It was plainly seen now that water had been at work for centuries, covering older floors and leaving new top surfaces; upon which later, roaming tribes settled.

After cleaning this level out another drop was made to five feet, which took us farther back under the sloping foundation. Spawls were plentiful here and showed more crude percussion breakage. A lava mortar, two pestles, a large, thin metate and hide scrapers were taken out. These were but a prelude to findings then unknown.

The lay of these primitive encampments was substantially established by this time. No mistake, plenty of hard, but pleasing work lay ahead. It was little short of a miracle that we worked here at intervals for so long without interference from well meaning, outside, inquisitive people. I have come back only to find previous openings shoveled full, and leads completely obliterated, —not a pleasant sight.

As work progressed on the three known floors of widely separated prehistoric periods it soon became evident that all dwellers, regardless of time, had used the same firepit buildup. Ashes, charcoal, burned bone and charred wood ends were found from top to bottom in the extended, rocked up pit. Our deep undercut trench had lengthened to thirty feet, and several fine artifacts were uncovered along the way. More pestles, moccasin forms, an arrow straightener, buckskin drying stones, a tomahawk head and arrowheads were the most important items taken from the five to six foot deep trench. All were very tightly pressed under and against the base; in fact, one pestle and mortar was crushed.

This is not an unusual occurrence in massive rim formations. The slight settling cannot be seen from decade to decade, but after thousands of years, the action is noticeable, as seen here. I have found, in two eastern Oregon rimrock formations, clear examples of this shifting and settling. One was a crushed metate between the sides of a rim rift, the other a flattened mortar beneath a cave wall. The earth's crust is constantly subjected to some degree of shock. Earthquake action, thunder jolts, volcanic eruptions, etc. are the ones within our range of sensitivity; but millions of minute vibrations go unnoticed. Anything natural bears no phenomenal implications.

In June, 1962, our deep trench was extended twelve feet more on the west end, and in this extension an unbelievable nest of artifacts was uncovered. The mortar, red lava pestle and forty-two primitive points were stimulating enough to a couple of tired diggers; but when the four fine old stone axes, two paint pots, with two four inch pestles inside came out—well, this was just about too much to bear. The colorful shades of jasper points had dimmed with age, and were crudely made in comparison to those found in upper floors. Figs. 74-76 and 77 show the heavier relics.

Figs. 78, 79 and 80 are from three overlaid levels. Each represents an evolutionary shift of styling from the Archaic Ages to a later prehistoric period, very unusual in one habitation site.

The little paint pots and pestles still retained the color pigments, red and yellow. It is amazing how this stain clings to damp, underground rock surfaces for thousands of years. Petroglyph painting has withstood weathering on rock faces for centuries. This primitive work of art is sometimes defaced and destroyed by selfish individuals, trying to chisel off a portion for their personal collections. Speaking in terms of the buckaroo camp, "my dander is easily raised," when it comes to destroying things the primitive will make no more.

In September, 1962, an additional number of artifacts was found, nearly seven feet deep. Four more ancient axes brought the grand total to eight. There seemed to be quite a demand for these blades in this earliest habitation. All were side grooved, for handle securing. When completed, this made them a necessary implement in splitting out arrow-shafts, pounding meat, breaking bones for the marrow, tool stock, killing a wounded animal, and last but not least, the perfect thing for putting a new part in an enemy's scalp or giving him a permanent anesthetic.

Mattock type digging tools found here were well constructed for their purpose. Long pointed blades were grooved for handles, slightly curved and brought to a flattened hoe edge on the opposite end. There was much use for this implement, digging out bulbs and tubers, herb roots and especially (we have learned from our generation of Indians) great quantities of fine textured tree roots were dug up and stored for basket and matting weaving. Others are made similar to our present day pointed, steel pick. Some smaller chisel shapes and spikelike pieces were used without handles.

There was no obsidian at this depth. These very early dwellers didn't seem to possess this stone from east of the Cascades, or leave any indication of having made contact with the Eukishikni (People of the Lake) just over the mountain divide. Possibly, they had migrated to this location from the northwest and were earlier than tribal infiltration along the eastern slopes of the Cascades.

Archaeologists and Geologists are making constant studies of the backtrails of early man migrations, but as yet there is insufficient evidence to warrant more than a reasonable deduction. This hesitancy is seen in writings such as that of Charles Miles, graduate of the University of California: quoting a line "However, it is believed by Archaeologists and Geologists that men must have crossed from Asia at the same time that many now extinct animals were passing to and fro over the land bridge that once existed between Asia and America."

Continental tribal migrations seem to be somewhat inconclusive even to regional movements, but a few definite facts have come out of this prehistoric habitation. The large amount of various artifacts verifies a progressive, intelligent and capable people. For every need there was a tool or implement; from green hides to soft garments, from nature to food mortars, from timber to the bows and arrows with which the primitive hunter filled his quiver.

This fascinating site was (I say was, for it has since been destroyed by road equipment) within thirty-five miles of our thickly populated Rogue Valley. A number of relic hunters had previously scouted over it, but failed to follow on through. Inward satisfaction compensated many times over for the tons of dirt thrown out.

There were no skeletal remains found, which is usual in cave diggings. If any one of the three widely separated habitations did not practice cremation rites, then it is quite possible to find their burials down along the creek banks.

From the findings, (and things not found) in the lowest floor of this site, we arrive at one convincing conclusion. These people were not affected by any outside influences. One would expect the Klamath Lake to be strongest, but there was nothing to indicate any contact. The Central and Northwest California should be second strongest, but screenings revealed nothing in the nature of personal adornment, nose plugs, ear spools, ear plugs, earrings, or any object of ornamentation. There were no signs of shell trinkets, dentalia, shell beads or engraved bone, eliminating any influential contact with the coastal people. Therefore, the only feasible analysis is that this lone tribe of primitive wanderers roamed into the secluded hunting grounds, dwelt for a time, and independently clung to their chosen way of life.

Moccasins no longer tramp the dust down around these smoke-stained dwellings, and the last sounds of life have filtered out beyond canyon walls and towering peaks. However the pictorial findings recorded on the spot, and the step by step explanation of procedures may perhaps bring back this Indian frontier, as closely as it can be reconstructed.

Figs. 73, 74, 75 and 76. *Above, left:* An overhang is not a cave, but exactly what the word implies. This one, on Little Butte Creek, has hovered for ages over the rich finds shown in Figs. 74 to 85, inclusive. *Right:* Stone axes, or tomahawk blades came from six feet below rim shown above. They are white flint, volcanic lava and basalt. All show equally fine work on differing compositions of stone. *Below, left:* Mortar, pestles, metate top (holding axe head), arrowshaft tools, hide tanning tools and moccasin lasts. *Right:* Hammers were essential implements in the Indian camps. The top three were for general use, such as driving stakes. The bottom two were used for lighter needs, such as bone cracking. All from Jackson County, Or.

Fig. 77. Rare axes and 4 inch paint pots with pestles. Red and yellow stains still clung to the mortars and pestles. Jackson County, Or.

Fig. 78. These heavy 2 to 4 inch obsidian points, of Rogue River Tribe design, were found in the uppermost level of habitation. The 16 x 20 inch lava metate came from the third level down. Jackson County, Or.

Fig. 79. The second level of habitation (down 3 feet) was a typical Rogue Indian camp. It yielded shorter points with long top barbs. Jasper, agate and obsidian ones were among the finest. Jackson County, Or.

Fig. 80. From the lowest level of habitation, 5½ to 6 feet deep, came this fine lot of crude but colorful points. They reveal a more primitive origin than the upper level finds. Jackson County, Or.

Figs. 81, 82, 83 and 84. *Above, left:* Author demonstrates how trenching, 40 feet long and 6 feet deep under cliff face led to the prized artifacts. *Right:* Deep trenching, always back and under, was continued along the wall. As the author found the relics, they were very carefully removed and tagged. *Below, left:* Lengthwise view of the 40 foot trench, showing how the wall was followed down and under. Note angle of shovel handle. *Right:* Artifacts found at the base of this massive overhang tell the full story of Indian activities. A leaning pole frame with a skin cover made them a home secure from storms, here. All, Jackson County, Or.

"Where Him Is, But Ain't"

Digging in these old cave depths I am often reminded of something my Indian friend Jim told me, when asked if he thought I could find an arrowhead up there in the overhang above the ranch house.

This being 1903, I had a lot of catching on to do. He said, "Go look where him is, but ain't—him down there alright." This is just about the best lesson in Archaeology I ever had. I have given it much thought, many times, when tempted to give up after a day's work without success. Then came that voice of old Indian Jim "Him down there alright" and renewed efforts paid off. This fine old fellow had made plain there are arrowheads, but not on top where you can see them. Dig down and you will find them. They are there, all right.

The overeager amateur collector must learn there will be days of disappointment, and spirits far below par; but when that first relic comes out he will mop off a dirty, sweat streaked face, smile to himself and contend that sore, aching muscles never felt better. A shovel in one hand and a pocketful of hope is a hard combination to beat.

Should there be a question in one's mind as to whether the darkened ceiling of a cave or overhang is smoke smudge or mineral stain, a chip can usually be chiseled or hammered off to see how deep the coloring matter is in original base rock. Smoke blackening affects only the surface; whereas mineral stain continues to penetrate.

As a word of caution to those unfamiliar with cave formations, I might make it clear that all are not safe to work in. Son-in-law Herb and I worked one out, in 1969, in the Klamath River canyon, where literally hundreds of tons of ceiling rock hung, suspended only by side wedge slabs, under a tremendous strain. A heavy jar or pried out rock could very well have dropped the whole thing.

This is no place for horseplay. There are horizontal, natural fractures in many age-old formations where water seeps in. This seam slowly expands with severe freezing, and over a period of undetermined years the ceiling is forced open and downward, which in due time drops to the cave floor. In this particular cave the loose overburden, from one to two and one-half feet thick and cracked throughout, has sagged until one can run an arm into the opening. When it finally lets go it will cover the tons of rock on the floor from previous falls. Menacing formations such as this one over one's head are not nerve comforters; but archaeological research warrants the taking of risks.

Lake County Cave

My last major cave exploration was in 1967 in northern Lake County, Oregon. In this one, my attention was centered on a roughly perpendicular crevice extending from the floor to the outside top. It was around two feet wide and went twenty feet back to a very good looking smoke outlet. Following ashes down, at the junction of the cave proper and the crevice base, a built-up flat rock wall or fire retainer was discovered across the crevice, just in back of the ash firepit. This was interesting, for human hands had placed those flat rocks there, apparently to keep fire away from what might be in the crevice.

I crawled in and began taking out dust and spawled off rock with no respirator on. Naturally, my nose became clogged, eyes reddened and watered, voice rasped incoherently, and an off-colored gray tongue licked at dry lips. At moments like this many convince themselves there is nothing down there in that choking ash and dust, pull out and look for an easier find. I'll admit these were almost my sentiments, but the only way to know if a specimen rests beneath the next inch of dirt is to tough it out.

All the while, that natural smoke chimney seemed to be most important. It leaned out about twenty feet, making a perfect draught column; with an outside pole and skin windbreak, the setting was great for a good cave dwelling. After a fresh air breath or two, troweling and shoveling was continued. Then came that old, familiar quartzite spearhead. An excited jump to rush outside (to tell my wife that I had strong suspicions of a cache coming up) reminded me that a human scalp has no business with those low, jagged lava pinnacles.

Immediately back, and twelve to eighteen inches deeper, sixty eight bone and stone working tools and implements were carefully removed from a recess behind a large slab of rock. They were in a good state of preservation, for no water or moisture of any kind could ever reach them.

Tangible evidence here points out higher developed skills in the construction of necessary tools and implements than was found in the Little Butte Site; but, like those people, no evidence of outside influences was detected. These Great Basin people were probably the same, or near neighbors of, the 9000 year primitives who were associated with the bark sandals, basketry, grass rope, etc., found in nearby caves. We are very much interested in new discoveries, for they enlarge our field of comparative values. Facts eliminate runaway theories. Stone artifacts were: rotation bow and shaft drills, punches, hide fleshers, thin cutting knives and finger awls. Bone tools consisted of punches, lacing and weaving tools, (two of which still have bits of buckskin in the eyelets) sinew or hair braiding separators, needles and a few unidentified objects.

After looking over the artifacts in Fig. 85 to 90, inclusive, one can envision the enormous amount of various articles fashioned with them. Secondly, picture the dugouts, gliding to wooded hunting shores; from cave dwelling to cave dwelling over waters they little dreamed would one day vanish.

Deep ash buildups have many times revealed as much of the prehistoric as artifacts themselves. In those five feet and deeper, one finds large pieces of charcoal showing the grain in heavy timber that had to come from somewhere else. We now see caves from a few miles out, to great distances from the timbered shores of prehistoric waters; stacked with driftwood and fallen trees, much the same as along ocean beaches. No doubt these early tribesmen used dugouts to tow logs and rafts loaded with heavy pieces to their cave homes, if deep deposits of large chunks of charcoal are any indication. In this particular ash deposit, which was some six foot deep, the uppermost two to three feet showed all fine textured ash left from burning brush type wood, such as sage and greasewood. One would be quite correct in saying these later period fires were used after the drying up period, and brush growth was creeping in over the whole area.

Lava Upheavals

Buttes and lava upheavals in the vast , wild area, east of the Cascade Range, have revealed more of the oldest artifacts, from the deepest penetration into unknown millenniums, than any western region I have had occasion to work in.

In 1967, an unexpected discovery of four Folsom type projectiles was made in northern Lake County. I had passed by, and studied this particular upheaval many times over the past forty years; having my family and friends along on this outing, it seemed an opportune time to go down into the old crevice.

The twenty foot wide bench in front seemed a natural lookout for the aborigine to sit and watch across the waters, for animals feeding on lush shores. The setting was just above the old water line, as shown by pebbles and bits of pumice washed in by waves. If any artifact, for any reason had been laid up, this was the only reasonable spot.

It was a tough one to clean out, as I had to work sideways in the narrow crack, and mostly head downward. It was an afternoon of trowel and finger scratching, all the time passing dirt out alongside my body. Near nightfall, the projectiles were found laying side by side, on edge, pressed tightly under a wedged in, crude metate. The points are from 2½ to 3½ inches long, with nice fluting, and made from a mottled, quartzite stone entirely foreign to this area. Knowing nothing of their origin, we are entitled to speculate that they were carried to this table-topped fortress by a drifting band of primitive hunters, following the second glacial ice recession.

However, the four projectiles thought to be Folsom have three characteristics identified with the Clovis point. They are larger, less finely flaked, and their bases show little or no earlike projection. On the other hand, the long, longitudinal side flakes removed are typical Folsom; as is the concave base, leaf shape and flaking. There is some difficulty in accurately placing an occasional point, for the trails of ancient man did not start and stop abruptly at any given time. Centuries may be involved in the overlapping periods.

The Sandia precedes both the Folsom and Clovis, being placed at more than 25,000 years old. They have no confusing similarity to the two mentioned. They are longitudinally notched at the base, forming a single shoulder; while the opposite edge is slightly rounded from point to the flat, rounded or concave base top. In other words, they are much like a wide leafshape with an elongated notch removed from one side at the base.

Archaeological findings seldom penetrate beyond the Folsom range of 10,000 to 25,000 years, or the Clovis, identified as the 10,000 to 13,000 year period.

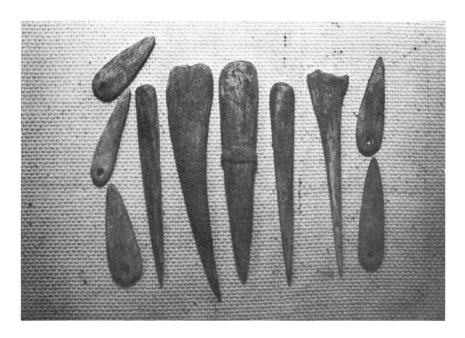

Fig. 85. Bone tools from the Lake County Cave, 1967. The five with holes in the large end were used to tie in ends of long hair, thus preventing tangling while braiding, etc.

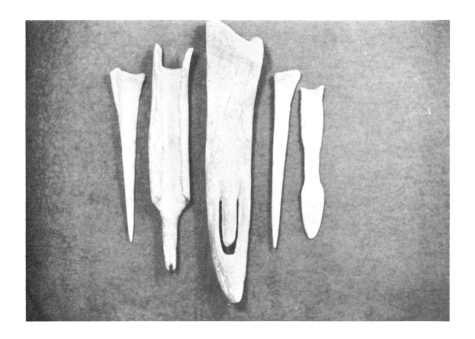

Fig. 86. More bone tools from cave cache, above. These were located in a crevice under 2 feet of ashes, dust and rock fragments.

Fig. 87. Fascinating variety of bone tools from Lake County Cave, 1967. The cache yielded 68 relics, including stone and bone knives, needles, drill, punches, fleshers, etc.

Fig. 88. Thin obsidian knives, used for working buckskin. Lake County Cave, 1967.

96

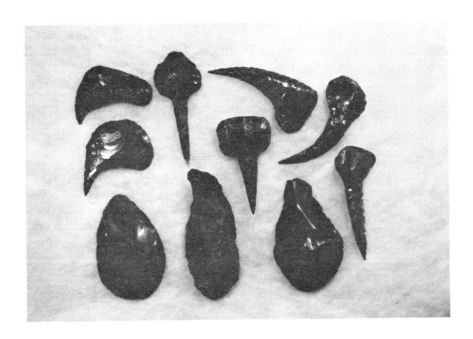

Fig. 89. Stone punches and fleshers. Lake County Cave, 1967.

Fig. 90. Bow and shaft drills; ancient hole makers in wood and stone. Drill was secured to shaft end. With cord wrapped a full turn around shaft, the bow was pulled back and forth, spinning the drill. Lake County Cave, 1967.

Fig. 91. The Folsom projectile is identified by the groove down each side, almost from top to point. Lava upheaval yielded these. Lake County, Or.

Fig. 92. Both of these Folsom type projectiles (and those above) are made from a stone similar to quartz, but not common in this area. Lava Upheaval, Lake County, Or.

Fig. 93. Unusual cave explored by author and family in 1958. About 250 feet in, it narrows to an impassable point; a room lies deep within. Overlooking the Clearwater River. Douglas County, Or.

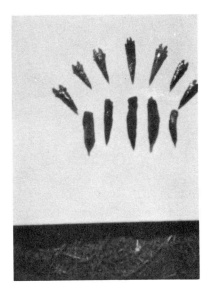

Fig. 94. Caves such as this one and the very deep one pictured above are easily passed by. In this cave I found my only Shoshone points and rotation type bow drills. *(Left)* Douglas County, Or.

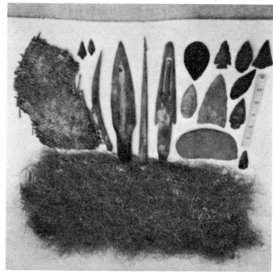

Fig. 95. Black obsidian spearheads, arrowheads and other stone pieces came into author's collection from this 36 foot deep lava cave. Lake County, Or.

Fig. 96. A variety of things turn up in Oregon Desert caves. Here are points, grass (reed) working tools, a basket segment, crude knife and a fibre mat—probably used for cradle padding. Lake County, Or.

Fig. 97. A section of the many petroglyphs painted on the underside of an overhang. Moss growth is gradually covering this ancient Indian art. Douglas County, Or.

Fig. 98. Overhanging art gallery. A section of the display is shown above. Located above the North Umpqua River, near Eagle Rock. Douglas County, Or.

Chapter IV
PACIFIC SHELL DOMAIN

CHAPTER IV

PACIFIC SHELL DOMAIN

This vast western land affords a great opportunity to study early Indian life and artifacts from a widely contrasting range of various locations. One of the most interesting and colorful is that of the shell domain of Pacific coastal dwellers.

The majority of us think of the beaches as a vacation land of swimming, suntans, and the ideal place to experience a campout near the pounding breakers. By choosing our time, we usually enjoy the outing as planned. Indian habitations here were compelled to weather out severe cold winds, violent downpours and thick, cold fog; often descending without warning. Those natives of the beach were a hardy lot to survive these extremes of nature.

Their shelters were constructed from any material that would shed water and blunt the wind. Excavations show the centers were dug out and banked around the outside with dirt and rocks. Driftwood poles were probably put up in the form of a tepee; covered with skins, slabs of bark, grass or a thick buildup of more poles. Two shelter remains showed that logs had been placed in squares similar to log cabin walls. A covering over this would provide a warm log dugout and protection from storms. Whatever the available material, little or no protection came from the easterly mountains' big timber, rimrock formations, or hot valleys beyond.

Ancient shell mound campsites and huge bakepits were usually found out on open, exposed banks, flats or sandy beaches just back from tidal runins. Scanty evidence showed shelter entrances to be on the easterly side, logical of course, because of the cold, prevailing winds coming in off the ocean. However, these conveniently located sites were close to their natural food basket, the ocean, which set no limits of food or variety.

I have asked old Indian friends of coastal areas if suffering from exposure and hardships were as we picture them, and the unanimous answer comes forth "We would not have had it otherwise." They loved this natural, rugged life they were born to and wanted no sympathy from anyone.

This personal aspiration to be classed separately as native coast people became a problem to government agencies, when they were trying to segregate the Klamaths for placement on the inland KlamathReservation.

Sometime back, I found this to be true in a conversation with a fine old Indian woman then living at the Smith River Reservation, near the California and Oregon border. When asked if she was a Smith River or Yurok, she said, "No, I'm a Klamath by birth. You see, when the soldiers came to take my mother back to Klamath, she said 'No, I'm a Smith River,' and she got to stay here; and here I've been all the time."She said her mother would choose to die before being dragged away from the ocean.

Shell Mound Digging

When searching for the Indian's handwork among the huge shell deposits, one automatically lays aside all thoughts of the desert country, caves, mountains and lakes of the interior. For it is here that we concentrate on shell ornaments of many descriptions: beads, bone tools, shell novelties, bone pendants and other things too numerous to list. There are some fine points, stone punches, hide scrapers, etc., but not in sizeable numbers.

It is very necessary for one exploring in these ancient mounds to work slowly and have a previous knowledge of how to remove and preserve the fragile works. It is most important to have some conception of how to handle the tons of shell and dirt without doing injury to these rapidly disintegrating artifacts. As a possible guideline, I have explained in this chapter many things that may be of benefit to those in doubt, and who might need just a little experienced help.

There were many small tribes living up and down the Pacific Coast within recognized borders, and we find it difficult to distinguish one from the other by artifacts found. Handwork arts and designing of ornaments and implements are very similar throughout the land of shell campsites.

If the coastal Indian friends we have known personally (several of whom have put a century of years behind them) reflect the lives of their ancestors, (which we have no reason to disbelieve) we must accept them as a gentle, trustworthy and non-aggressive people.

Four Fathers

Many years ago I had my hat set back by an old blood at Brookings, Oregon, when I asked what he thought of his forefathers. Somewhat ruffled, he said "Meybe you got four fathers, Injun only got one. Too much fathers, too much mixum up." This taught me how easy it is to climb out on a brittle limb.

Screening is advisable in shell deposits where there is evidence of beads or small trinkets. I find a 3/8 inch square mesh most suitable for this purpose; too many pieces pass through a larger size, while too little material can be put through in a day if it is smaller.

Inland and northerly from the California Bay Area, old campsites and burials show a heavy trading with coastal tribes for any form of the shell family. Knolls along sloughs, river banks, and especially at the confluence of two streams, such as the Feather and Yuba Rivers, we look for signs leading to a prehistoric camp. Flood waters may have washed out or built up these promising locations some three to six feet. One need not be surprised or confused at finding distinct layers of dirt, gravel and sand in the downward excavation. I have never worked one of these locations that didn't contain various shell ornaments and bone tools.

Tooth Shell (Dentalium)

The tooth shell (dentalium) was an ornament highly valued by all western tribes. Its worth was early discovered by tribal traders, as evidenced by its wide distribution; at

Fig. 99 This photo shows the bottom 3 feet of a 7 foot cut through a shell mound. Note packed dirt, shells and firepit stones. Curry County, Or.

Fig. 100 Reward of three days of careful work in the above site. Stone pestle, boat or net weight, grooved hammer, punches, bone arrowheads, bone head effigy, harpoon, fork, spoon, bone hair pins (6-12 inches long) and carved cup. Curry County, Or.

Fig. 101. At a depth of approximately 4 feet this (more recent) mound of camp midden gave up an interesting relic of ox and team days. Del Norte County, Ca.

Fig. 102. From the diggings above came two cast iron kettles, rusted tightly together. Their bottoms were recessed, to use on an iron ring above campfires. They were common in wagon trains, early in the 19th century. Possibly they were prized loot from an Indian raid on an early settler. Del Norte County, Ca.

least as far as the Dakota-Montana border, where I have found them. They have been mistakenly called tusk, horn, snail, etc., as they do indeed slightly resemble such shapes. They are actually ocean shells, once containing a living creature. Their average length is 1 to 2 inches, 1/8 to 1/4 inch diameter at the large end, tapering off to almost a point at the small end. Longer ones have been seen on antique chief regalia. After the creature was boiled out of these eye catching ornaments, they were often made even more beautiful by engraving, painting or polishing.

Past accounts reveal that a young brave with two or three dozen polished dentalium was assured of a trade for a new wife. Of course, we have no information on whether the smaller amount was good for a small one, or the larger number good for a large woman; but evidently they were a practical substitute for wooing, or demonstrations of physical strength.

The Nootkans claimed for a time to be the only tribe capable of retrieving these shells from the Pacific depths. The Oregon Indian and Haida claimed they obtained their decorations from dead ones along the beaches. We are amazed by the Indian's ingenious contraption devised to retrieve shell ornaments from the ocean floor. After the bed was located, and if the water was not too deep, pole after pole was lashed together until the bottom was reached. Secured to the bottom pole end was a round, broomlike trap made from cedar splinters; finer ones in the center and coarser ones on the outside layers, all wrapped tightly, near the top. This would appear small and compact next to the pole and flared out at the bottom. A slab of wood with a hole large enough to slip over the top of the broom, with rock weights secured on each end, worked as a squeeze on the lower section of broom, when gigged up and down. The long pole assembly was then jabbed against the bottom several times, to press the tubular, perpendicular shell creature into the splinter broom. The rock weights jarred down, forming a squeeze that tightly held the well earned dentalia. If luck held and the waves didn't snap the lashed poles, the dentalium fisherman came up with a few valuable trade items, desirable, to the inland tribes. Similar dentalia have been retrieved in fossil formation from rock used for new road construction in Jackson County, Oregon, verifying their millions of years of existence.

Whaleshead Shell Mound

In 1958, I met Max Brainerd of Brookings, Oregon, a man who possessed great knowledge of early Indian and White activities. He was gracious enough to ride with me to the mountains, where he pointed out the location of an ancient Indian site far below, at Whaleshead Rock; then inaccessible to vehicle travel. I packed in there and made some valuable finds of primitive artifacts, partially shown in Fig.100.

This wild, rough Whaleshead Coast borders the land once held by the Wishten-atan Tribe, ending at Arch Rock on the north. There began the domain of the Chetl-essentan Tribe, running on north to Hunters Head. To the south of the Wishten-atan, approximately half way between the Chetco River and Hasontas River (now called the Win-

105

chuck) ruled the Chetco Tribe. In their village site on the west side of Chetco River, bordering the ocean, the artifacts in Fig. 103 were found. South of the Chetcos, the Hasontas ruled into northern California; but not overlapping the lower Klamath River People.

It was in Hasontas territory, Del Norte County, that I opened up the shell mound shown in Fig.107. Light material, foreground, is all shell from bakepits. The buildup here was enormous. Various specie of clam, mussel, barnacles and just about any ocean creature that lived in a shell, including snails, were sorted out.

Coastal tribes showed little interest in the Coastal Range and, as the mountains rose higher, their interest definitely faded out. One exception was the Shas-te-koos-tees, who held to the banks of the To-To-Tu-Na (Rogue River) up as far as the confluence of the Illinois and Rogue, where their farthest village east was located. It seems strange that the Shas-te-koos-tees didn't demand a few miles of ocean frontage. There was only about three miles between their western border and the beach line. However, for unknown reasons they seemed to have settled for the small strip starting three miles inland, up the north and south sides of the To-To-Tu-Na, bordering the Euquachees, north, and the Yahshutes, south.

A seven foot face in the shell mound, Fig. 89, is shown for a specific reason. It is now ready to start work on from the bottom up, a method found to be much more satsifactory than digging from the top down. This saves many fragile pieces, as shell and camp refuse caves off from the trowel point, underneath. It is not advisable to remove more than a foot of face to the top at a time; thus avoiding cave ins that crumple the artifact you so much wanted to save.

Crescent City Shell Mound

Wagon train cast iron kettles, Fig.102, found four feet deep in a shell mound near Crescent City, California, are evidently sad reminders of Indian raids on a pioneer home or covered wagon traveler. They were nearly eaten away by rust, and were resting in a large, rocked in bakepit. Their being so out of place makes one both hesitate and wonder.

Figs. 101 and107 picture typical shell mounds after being opened up. One finds it educational, interesting and surprisingly invigorating to work in one of these old bake sites; making notations, looking over various species of shell life and hoping to see a fine piece of bone work slide down from among the shells. Here, Indians lived and pre-pared ocean foods for centuries, as kicked over refuse on the banks show. Another attraction is the display of half and whole shells still intact that make colorful collection exhibits. Now and then an abalone shell shows up and they polish nicely.

An occasional mound site is built up to eight or ten feet from the original base where the first bakepit was constructed. Evidence shows, in these massive ones, they were a much used, congregating spot in the lodge when fresh bags of new catches came in. Circular shapes are the natural result of squatted groups finished off the hot contents, and tossed the empty shell wherever convenient.

Alongside one ancient mound there appeared to be the rotted remains of two old

106

Fig. 103. The harpoon in center of photo is an extra fine specimen. It has a stone head, bone shank and wooden handle. The hair pins *(below)* are rare. The fine art of bone working is seen in all of the artifacts.

Fig. 104. This 4" x 15" stone pestle shows by its design and weight (for instance, the cone shaped base) to have been used as a rotating crusher, rather than a pounding instrument. San Joaquin County, Ca.

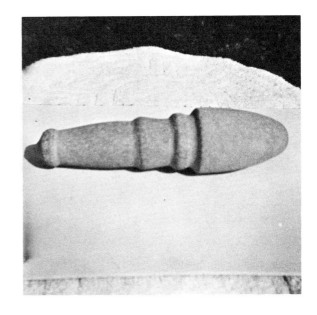

107

Fig. 105. A 22 inch bone metate, or all around dish. It has been scooped out to a depth of 3 inches. The specimen had to be repaired and sealed before it could be removed from its resting place, the second day. Curry County, Or.

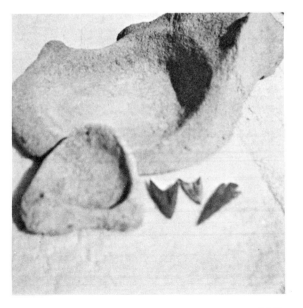

Fig. 106. These dishes were probably made from whalebone. Bone arrowheads reflect more of the fine art. These are from a shell mound in Curry County, Or.

Native Seafood Kitchen

Fig. 107. Ancient shell mound campsite on the extreme northwest Pacific Coast of California. A buildup of refuse, sea shells and layers of firepit rock and dirt; we now see only a brush covered knob that once smelled richly of baked clams and racks of nae-pooie (smoked salmon). This particular camp concealed under heavy brush and foliage, was approximately nine feet deep, a typical shell mound.

Despite their value to coastal archaeology these old bakepits are becoming much more difficult to document; whatever prehistoric purpose they may have served, they are presently being indiscriminately destroyed. New roads, housing developments, private interests and commercializing of shell beds for crop fertilizing all work toward this end. Such is progress. Del Norte County, Ca.

109

dugouts, and log foundations of either shelters or food storages.

With all things taken into consideration, I find the primitive shell mound a most fascinating place to explore. It has been my experience to find few arrowheads, which seems to verify that their fishing was mainly done by the use of nets, seines, traps or baited bone hooks on sinew lines. Probably there were many contraptions we are not familiar with.

Historic articles tell us that when the white man first looked in upon these coastal tribes he quickly realized they were content, interested little in things beyond their borders and perfectly happy in their hereditary brotherhood of Pacific Thanksgivings.

A personal friendship with many descendants has added a certain luster to my explorations into the prehistoric activities.

Preserving Fragile Pieces

Some bone work found in this Pacific shell mound country is in the last stages of disintegration, but can generally be saved if one takes time to figure the possible angles, and works slowly.

This was the case in the fine old bone metate seen in Fig.105. The scooped out bone dish was 22 inches long, and at first there seemed little hope of removing it intact, as it had already cracked apart in over a dozen places. It lay about 4 foot deep in the outer edge of a large shell mound at the Chetco River mouth, Brookings, Oregon. I wanted this fine old relic, and walked round and round, trying to figure a way to hold those loose pieces together. Finally, the shell and dirt was carefully brushed and blown from the top, leaving the bottom undisturbed in its firm shell pack, underneath.

I had gone fully prepared on this trip, as always, with material to remove and to preserve just such fragile relics. Thus, I was ready to work on the interesting job ahead. After the cracks were well cleaned out, a pan of water-mix-hard rock putty was prepared. Yellow clay was added to match old bone color. The thin mixture was worked into the dozens of cracks and crevices, smoothed off and left to set until the second day. The work looked fine the next morning, but I knew the next few seconds would tell whether the old bone relic could be lifted out. It came out of its "nest" in one piece. After being turned bottom up it was given the same treatment on the other side. It was next sprayed several times with plastic air sealer, and another valuable old bone relic was saved, intact.

Sincere collectors will utilize the method described in this setting, to remove and preserve fine old relics that would otherwise crumble into a total loss.

Another good specimen of heavy bone utensil is seen in Fig.106. This one and the smaller bone tray seem to be whalebone, and are fairly solid. Bone arrowheads in the same picture have also retained their polished surface.

In the beautiful pestle, Fig.104, we again see an extraordinary touch in workmanship typical of these Pacific Shell People. In stone designs, shell carving or bone arts we see a highly skilled outlet for a personal desire for something eye catching, perfect and neat; just a little better than the ordinary.

The bone work viewed in Fig.103 reflects more of the skill in these primitive hands. We must remember that all of these fine artifacts were shaped and smoothed by nothing more than sharp edged rock chips, stone drills, sanding stones, sand and hard shell. A few show signs of fire being used to burn away excess length and outside fullness.

In this picture we see, from top to bottom, a large awl or punch; harpoon head; cup made from a vertebra; large spoon; stone head harpoon; hair pins; arrowheads; fork and weaving tools. The harpoon is a prized work of ingenuity. The round bone base is neatly fitted to a stone head, with wooden shaft inserted in the other end; but the real cleverness lies in the barb. The bone base is cut out so the barb can work freely; then, a bone pin is run through holes in the base and barb, so that the barb can hinge in and out. It can partly close as the thrust is made into flesh, and then open up when a pull is made on the shaft or thong attached in the hole seen at the shaft end of the bone base. The balance of the shaft crumbled away with a shell slide before I realized it was a harpoon, intact.

We naturally deplore the loss of meaningful artifacts, destroyed by parties who dig recklessly or indiscriminately. Speed and a poor system have ruined many irreplaceable relics. Indiscreet handling and scanty knowledge of preservation methods account for the loss of others. Therefore, as a sincere personal request "How about making a study of those fast vanishing sources of ancient Indian lore, rather than expose them to wanton waste?"

Dormant Demons

There is an occasional day in the old shell mound excavation that arouses in one the dormant demon of Greek Mythology. One full day had been spent digging a large pit, six feet deep by about eight feet square. The next day around noon, six or eight bone artifacts began to show in one shell wall, requiring some delicate removal. I decided to go down to the beach and have lunch, first.

Upon returning, I found three fellows down in my pit shoveling and picking down the face, ruining every specimen in sight. With my temper soaring, I jerked out my pick handle, (to sort of square the odds) and said, "Now get going, and quick." My first and second demands were met with sneers, and signs of violence; but that drawn back pick handle must have looked rather uninviting for the big, defiant, mother's son cleared the top in nothing flat. Such an incident seldom occurs, for most spectators are respectful of one's digging operations.

Importance of Midden

Midden heaps along inland California river banks, such as the Sacramento, Feather, and Yuba, show the heavy use of river mussels, which were baked in the same manner as coastal shell life. The word "midden" arouses little interest, even among those searching for Indian lore. As tangible material, however, it offers clues to various phases in the lives of the prehistoric people associated with mound buildups. The word "midden" is

111

defined as a refuse dump. So it is, but it is also a reservoir of rich information about the site. The base material indicates a very remote age, and the layers of dirt floors spaced between layers of shell was probably the outcome of better footing requirements; when loose shell became too deep for comfort. I have traced five or six of these dirt floor fills over as many layers of shell in a single midden site. Findings are not theoretically based, for a top to bottom cut through the mound reveals such statements to be correct. A few bone and shell tools are found broken, as if they had been stepped on around the bake ovens; for both pieces will be laying end to end. These can be mended nicely, and make as valuable relics as they originally were.

Though we do our utmost to reconstruct camp activities from findings, an occasional one slips in unsolved. Screening out this particular camp refuse verified its being the trampled family cooking spot, where I expected to find little of value. To my surprise, in the outer perimeter of shell depths, I ran onto groups of the finest bone work, engravings, ornaments and unique pieces. Nine 8 to 10 inch ceremonial bone hairpins, (three engraved) and other fine relics seen in Fig.103 were among the lot. These must be seen to be believed.

The finding of those rare and beautiful artifacts is not too unusual; but in this instance, their location in the outer midden embankment simply puts us on the spot for an immediate answer. Solutions to some problems come slowly, for a number of puzzlers are in direct discord with what we know of the Indian's cunning practice in hiding or laying away his valued possessions. Deducing from various field experiences, this setting seemed to offer us a likely answer which perhaps may have more substantial bearing than we are aware of. It is quite possible that certain sections of the outer shell face were, as we might say, "roped off, and out of bounds" to camp travel. They are much easier to dig into than the trampled ground.

After working through, and observing all things in conjunction with these ancient shell sites, we are convinced that from one to several families used bakepits; according to the shell surface area. On the smaller ones, (fifteen to twenty five feet across) there is usually one oven found; while an elongated one of perhaps eighty feet across, on the Chetco River, showed fire rings conveniently spaced over most of the surface.

Feather and Yuba River Excavation

Displays in Figs.110 and 111 are from a seven foot excavation at the confluence of the Feather and Yuba Rivers, California. From under tree roots, hundreds of shell beads and disk wampum (or shell money) came out on the screen. The site was evidently a long used camp of the Wintun Tribe, and extended through midden to this depth. The habitation was a tough one to follow, due to scattered material and abrupt dropoffs on certain levels. Skeleton fragments and broken bone tools lay in confusing locations, which slowed work.

It came to me that this ground disruption was most likely caused by the river, which at some prehistoric time made an undercut; whereby the entire camp and burial grounds toppled to a lower location. At a later time this dirt was covered by a gravel

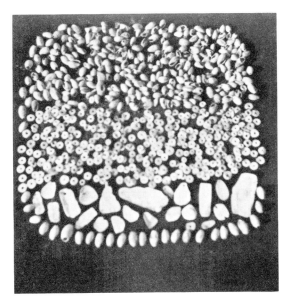

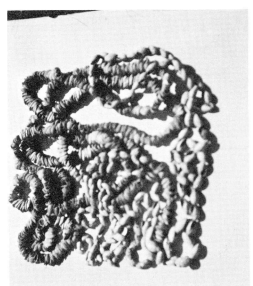

Fig. 108. The Feather River diggings turned out hundreds of olivela shell beads, round shell (wampum) beads, carved abalone shell and sundry other items. Sutter County, Ca.

Fig. 109. Yards of restrung olivela and cup shaped shell beads. Feather River diggings, Yuba City, Ca.

Fig. 110. Extremely hard mussel 4 to 6 inches long, were drilled for stringing and shaped as ornaments. With the outer film removed, they glow as richly as pearls. Curry County, Ca.

Fig. 111. Stone net weight and sinkers seem to be a part of the Shell People's culture all up and down the Pacific Coast. Most are roughly 2" to 4" in diameter. Curry County, Ca.

113

bar, which now presented a major problem in digging. Findings were usual, but a large cup of teeth screened out were sound evidence of the grinding, crushing and sliding of ground that had mangled skeletons and fragile bone artifacts.

A most unusual and interesting discovery of unique artifacts and customs of a primitive people living during a period of 2000 years or more ago can be viewed in Figs. 112, 113, 114 and 115. I have made a careful study of this burial of the prehistoric Yokut Tribesmen, (complete with drawn notations of positions) as hand excavation progressed.

It was through my daughter Yvonne and son-in-law Herb, I had been informed of artifacts being destroyed by a leveling project at this site. I was there the next morning, and to one whose aim it is to study and preserve our ancient man's work, the sight of skeleton fragments, crushed shell work and broken points scattered all about called for immediate action. Test holes were dug in one remaining section of the site; and here I made a discovery that contributed much to our meagre knowledge of the ancient Yokuts.

Work went on, at times under adverse conditions. Drenching rains poured down, and mud stuck to me in gooey gobs. But as long as fine artifacts were being found and preserved, every minute was a pleasure; such an opportunity seldom comes a second time. As heavy excavations continue to meet new housing and highway demands in the area northerly from Stockton, California, we may look for more sites left by the Yokut Indians. A recent discovery shows some artifacts belonging to this particular tribe as being carbon-14, dating back to nearly 1,000 B.C. In addition to their anthropological value, the abalone shell carvings were superb in every detail.

Fig. 112 and 113 show two of eight abalone necklaces saved from the excavation. Each shell is restrung in its original position, as found on the remains. We know this shell to be one of extreme hardness, and only by imagination can we partially grasp the patience, work and unlimited time put forth in these designs. Each piece is drilled for stringing and cut into the most unusual designs of pendants, beads, round discs, squares and medallions. Naturally, the sinew or hide lacings had disintegrated in ages past; but I devised a method by which the necklaces could be restrung in the same position as they were at time of burial.

This was done by laying each shell out on paper as it was removed and pencil drawing made around it, until all were out; giving me a complete drawing of the many shapes in the necklace and their original positions. This lot, with drawing, was placed in an individual container to be taken back for later reconstruction. Shells were layed over the sketch to fit, thus making it impossible to restring and design out of its original position.

Unique Shell Mound Burial

Throughout these burials there was clear evidence of a spiritual conception of a higher and greater power. Fig. 113 shows three skulls, with carved abalone medallions in place on the heads, as found in burial. The female, left, had a band of round medal-

114

lions around her head; female right, had intricately designed shells on either side of her head, with one over the top. The male, center, was found with one large medallion on either side of his head, covering the ear location. The three had been buried in unison, as seen by the overlapping of hands and arms, ruling out the possibility of three single burials. The bodies had been placed in a bended knee, sitting position with arms partly outstretched; two facing south, one facing north. In other words, facing each other.

A partial cremation ceremony was involved here, as all three skeletons showed definitely charred bone around the chest and top ribs; on one, the under chin was slightly burned. Final confirmation of a cremation having taken place was the charred remains of cremation baskets around each, made of reed or grass. It was quite easy to follow the charred wrapping of burned cremation baskets, and I managed to carefully remove several pieces to confirm the things I saw as part of this primitive ceremony.

The three skulls in Fig. 113 were removed intact, and preserved for future study by applications of Acrylic clear No. 1-10. Female left and male center were well along in years, while the female right would be considered a young woman by her set of fine, unworn teeth.

Another strange thing was noted in the burial of the three together. The male had a black obsidian disk in the roof of his mouth, and the older female had a flat stone bead in her mouth. Both females were buried with their cut shell necklaces, and there seemed no partiality between them, as far as ornaments were concerned.

Many questions arise here. Did the old chief (and I would say he was such by the special possessions with him and found in no other burial) have two wives? Did he die first and the tribe then put away his wives to unite the family again in the great Happy Hunting Grounds? What sort of primitive prayers spiraled upward in the smoke from this cremation ceremony?

Things seen in burials usually present a workable solution to understanding, but this group burial leaves us in some doubt as to the ancient Yokut's system of principles or rules; possibly better termed the tribal code.

These people seemed to have possessed a long life span, viewed from fragments of skulls scattered by machinery on the job. Worn teeth, many to the gum line, suggests most adults were far beyond their prime.

Preservation of Skulls

Many have been unable to remove and preserve these aged craniums for study after locating them, saying they fell apart and could not be saved. Dirt must be kept in contact with disintegrating skulls until their later removal, or all one will have is a heap of teeth and bone fragments. To save these, a thin box with an open top and bottom was placed around the skull and pressed in, as dirt from the back edges was dug away with a trowel. Mud was then packed into voids and the whole tipped forward, and carefully removed from the excavation; and again sealed with mud. It can then be taken out and wrapped with cloth, where it remains until taken home to slowly dry. When all dirt has

Fig. 112. Eight beautiful abalone necklaces were retrieved, saved from leveling operations. Each piece is painstakingly cut and drilled. Their original positions were traced on paper, and they were later restrung from the pattern. San Joaquin County, Ca.

Fig. 113. Three prehistoric skulls with abalone medallions recorded a unique burial ceremony of the primitive Yokut. San Joaquin County, Ca.

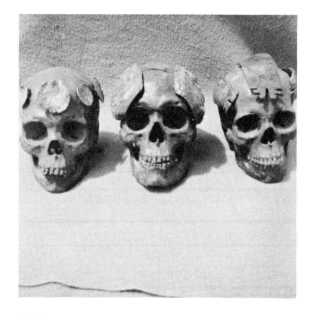

dried, a stiff brush is used to slowly work off same from outside surfaces. As the skull appears, apply several coats of plastic to set and harden. After the inside dirt is slowly worked out, pour in a half pint of shellac to reach all spots of the interior. One can now handle them carefully.

Using this procedure, we have removed and preserved intact craniums of the primitive, ranging into the 3000 year period. The abalone shell medallions were replaced in their original resting place, on the skull.

One burial showed signs of hot tempers in the old Yokut camp. This Indian had been crammed into a hole in no respectful manner, almost head down. A white arrowhead, found later, had entered the skull from above and behind, passing through the head and lodging under one eye. He was a young Indian, but that arrow stopped any notions he had of breaking the tribal code. These Yokut Indians were of medium build, and heavy boned.

After the findings here were studied and notes recorded the remains were placed in deep trenches below the leveling operation, where they will remain. Most of the single burials seemed to be women, with a cut shell necklace on and a pestle alongside.

One aged male was found, about five feet deep, with an estimated ten pounds of black obsidian spawls ranging from one inch to three inches in diameter, packed under his chin. They had been roughly flaked out, evidently for arrowhead making. The preliminary work was probably done far away, where he obtained the stone, to eliminate carrying excess weight on the long trip back. Before I left he was reburied deeper, as were the others. Possibly he is now resting beneath someone's lawn.

Only four skulls were preserved for future study; the specially adorned ones, that give us a little more factual knowledge of the primitive Yokut.

So, with the combined material and findings from three days of hard work, we conclude the tribe was unexcelled in the art of cutting hard abalone shell into intricate, ornamental designs for headbands and beautiful necklaces. They would savagely deal out justice to an enemy code breaker, verified by the arrowhead in the skull and broken limb bones found in one burial. Personal adornment was worn in the burial finals, concluded by a partial cremation ceremony. Cremation baskets revealed a beautiful touch in fine reed weaving, and the many symmetrical, roller type pestles showed an extra touch of personal ambition.

The rare Stockton, serrated arrowhead peculiar to this tribe is shown in Fig. 115. In other respects they seemed to have lived about the same as their brother tribes, the Miwok, Winton, Maidu or Costanoan. The Yokut findings are indicative of a lively, progressive and highly skilled people. Their primitive craftsmanship demonstrates their love of beautiful, personal adornment.

Then came a sad day to the Yokut, when the last fires were built over departing ones; and smoke ceased to spiral up and beyond to their Great Spirit's hunting grounds of plenty.

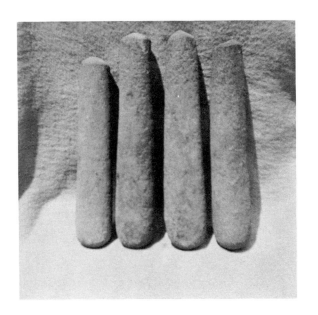

Fig. 114. Shown are four of ten roller type pestles found in the ancient Yokut burials. Diligent searching yielded no mortars or metates, however. San Joaquin County, Ca.

Fig. 115. Rare 2 to 3 inch Stockton points, found in Yokut burial. They seldom appear outside a 300 mile radius of Stockton, California. Their scarcity and extremity of design both point to personal high ambition on the part of the primitive that painstakingly designed them. San Joaquin County, Ca.

Fig. 116. Arrowheads are scarce in the shell domain, yet those found show marked skill in their construction. Stone in the vicinity offers red, brown, light green, white and gray varieties. Curry County, Or.

Fig. 117. This unique metate and pestle demonstrate the extra touch devoted to stone work by the Pacific Shell People. From Curry County, Or.

119

Whaleshead Cache

Figs. 120 and 121 show interesting work in carving and drilling bone, bear tusks and shell. This fine lot was discovered in a site originally occupied by an ancestral branch of the Chetco Tribe, at Whaleshead on the Pacific, Curry County, Oregon. I did camp tracing here, before new highway construction up the coast; the only trail then being from the old mountain summit road down over wild, rough, steep, almost inaccessible hills and gullies to the shell buildup.

After five years of intermittent searching and gathering of artifacts shown previously in this chapter, the cache containing these was found. Such discoveries should stimulate the efforts of lukewarm collectors. The presence of rare work found year after year should induce many to continue, by all means.

Picture, if you wish, my lonely camp down in this deep, isolated spot; hearing no sound, nor seeing any moving thing but the Pacific. Unmolested work and little regard to time was the main factor in finding and preserving over 300 artifacts from this old Chetco encampment. They are doubly appreciated today, as there will probably be no more explorations. The shell site is now within a state park. As the night fire pushed back an inevitable fog, appraisals were made of the day's find and I felt responsible to future interests in recording everything possible left by these talented people.

It was noted that bone fish net tools, lance heads, fish effigies and animal teeth were in a fair state of preservation. This points out the possibility of their being made within the past few generations. I am speaking now of the last major find in the figures above. The spearhead and arrowheads are of coastal stone, in off shades of blue, green, gray and brown. Most likely, the necklace of bear tusks, large teeth, fish effigies and moon crescents are memoirs of a proud hunter of the shadowed forest trails; or a fisherman of the briny depths. The carved, drilled and polished shell necklace is feminine in design, and represents many hours of patient work. Olivela beads and the highly valued dentalium added much to the find.

With some degree of luck, drawings and measurement locations of previous diggings, I was able to continue in the new ground, with no time lost. Deep shell deposits, with only broken and stray bone work were bypassed for the time. New test holes showed inside shelter fire pits, suggesting lodge locations to one side and near the protective cliff face; a natural hiding place between the rim and lodge for anything of value, should it be needed. A trench was started here, and continued at about two feet deep. In the late afternoon, in an approximately eight inch wide channel, between slabs of rock placed over and leaned up against the wall, this fine lot of relics was uncovered. These are moments that belong to and remain with the collector; though wanting to share them, writing fails to do them justice.

An extremely high tide had rolled in during the afternoon, cutting off my way out, forcing a climb up and over the rough top; but the packsack of tissue wrapped artifacts came to no harm.

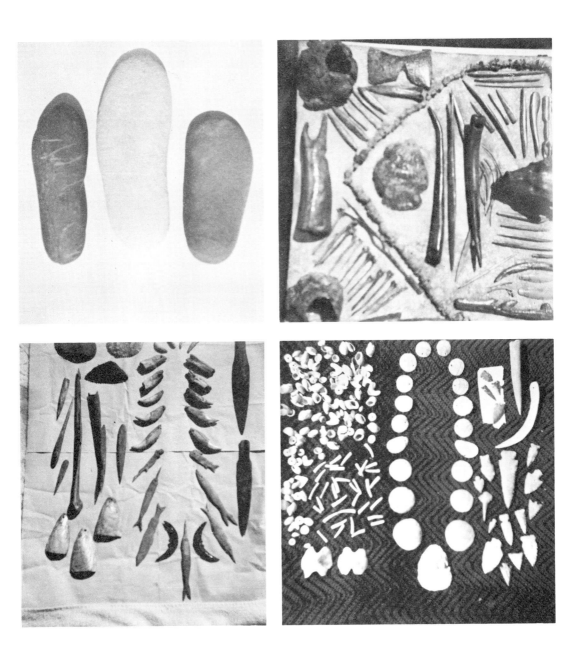

Figs. 118, 119, 120 and 121. *Above, left:* Stone moccasin molds were found in shell diggings, as in most western Indian habitations. Reversible, they served as forms for sewing either moccasin. A wet moccasin could be slipped onto the heated rock and dried to the proper shape, once again. *Right:* Bone work ranging from needles, punches and ornaments to trap sets and beads are found in most shell mounds along the Pacific Coast. *Below, left:* Artifacts from last exploration of Whaleshead Site. Carved bone fish effigies and bear teeth are believed to have formed a necklace. *Right:* Another group from the same site. Olivela beads, dentalium, drilled necklace shell, points and other pieces came from a depth of 2 feet, close to an abrupt rim facing the sea. Curry County, Or.

Fig. 122. The author's three daughters—June, Nadra and Yvonne—learn that rough, rain-gutted coastal slopes yield relics trapped when ancient banks caved in and washed toward the sea. The shot at left shows a 300-foot drop toward the beach.

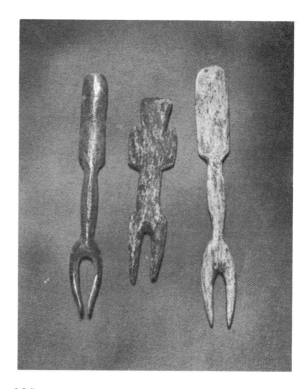

Fig. 123. These beautiful bone forks undoubtedly served the primitive such delicacies as baked clams and mussels. From Chetco and Whaleshead Sites, Curry County, Or.

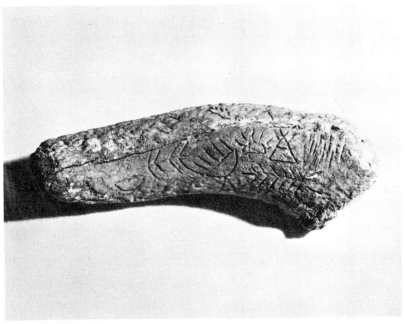

Figs. 124 and 125. *Above:* Bone and ivory, engraved by the Pacific Shell Mound Indians. These trinkets lay at depths from 5 to 7 feet. *Below:* Section of engraved elk horn. Most of the surface had decayed away. Curry County, Or.

These field experiences have been related within the bounds of my knowledge which, allowing for personal deliverance, should shed a much greater light upon the lives and activities of our western shell mound inhabitants.

Shaker's Convention

Existing descendants of those prehistoric natives, though fewer in number, still gather to celebrate certain festivities and hold church services. My wife, grandson Steve, granddaughter Karen and I were invited to attend one at Rivers End, Smith River Colony. We were very pleased to accept the special invitation to go into the Indian settlement to attend the Shaker's Religious Convention. This we had not previously experienced, and felt it quite an honor to be asked to the services. Long tables were prepared, and they shared with us their food and prayers. In the following hours we learned much from the lips of a fine people.

Those attending came from the lower Klamath River settlements of California, northward to Brookings, Oregon. We hold a growing admiration for these sincere Indian people, who so devotedly cling to the principles of their faith.

A small candle was lighted and placed in front of our plates; the soft tinkle of a little bell was heard in the background.

While eating, an elderly woman sitting across the table from us told of the origin and continuance of the Shaker religion, as passed down to them through many generations. There had been a great conversion from the primitive fires where self torture was inflicted and human sacrifices were offered as wild cries rent the air, to a gentle people of quiet church assemblies.

These humble folks offered prayers for their sick members and gave thanks for what they have, though little, in all earnestness. We were deeply impressed with the proceedings at this convention among our Indian friends, and value the welcome spirit shown by all present.

After a word of appreciation to Rev. Sivonen, "Mika Wash" to his brothers and sisters, a shoo-oo-nap-paah (goodbye my brother) to our good friend Seeley Griffin and a big smile to a bright little Indian baby strapped in a nau-ausk (papoose cradle) we departed with precious things to remember.

I know these people to be proud of their ancestors. They ask for nothing and have little, but are strong in their faith of a better day to come. To accept their lot is to enjoy peace of mind. If any harbor ill will toward their white neighbors, it is not shown. Mistrust, yes. This is seen in many Indian homes of today. A stranger not acquainted with the family quickly senses the coolness and by no means should they try to force a friendship upon the older generation. Early military personnel and other aggressive white individuals have left scars upon them that require more time to heal.

However, my family and I find our coastal Indian friends a fine people to visit and it is most heartening when my wife and I take leave to hear them say, "Choo-oo-nap-paah and choo-oo-nay-way," meaning "goodbye, my brother" and "goodbye, my sister."

124

Chapter V
SKYLINE SITE

CHAPTER V

THE SKYLINE SITE

Timbered water divides, spring dampened glades, river banks or valley floors force the artifact hunter to change his technique of exploration with each given location. Few works of art are seen on the surface in the land of mountains and valleys; which leads us underground with pick and shovel in the hopes of screening out relics.

Indians who lived in this beautiful environment of plenty enjoyed a peace hard to forfeit by command of the United States military, as reservation drives began. As stated in Chapter Two, there were thousands of personal possessions cached with hopes of one day coming back to them, the mountain regions being no exception.

In this Skyline Site cached articles prove the Indians' cunning by both their method of concealment and protective measures taken, to guard against destruction. Theirs was an inheritance of nature's bountiful display of grandeur in which they roamed at will.

A Night in the Big Woods

This came to me more clearly than ever one night in camp (on the upper Rogue waters) as I sat by the fire, meditating. In contrast to the hot, dustladen, windswept desert I sweltered in on previous hunts, I would like to share with you a moment of relaxation and beauty. Call it if you will "A Night in the Big Woods."

It was a late August midnight when I arrived in this moonlit river retreat; sweat streaked, grimy and footsore from the crunch, crunch over miles of blistering sand and cracked alkali I had left behind but a few hours ago. I slipped into the river for a washdown, while the old coffee pot brewed up a much needed lift to morale.

The enchantment of this silvery night enveloped my entire being. Higher in the canyon, softly far and yet so near, the stream's voice was faintly audible. Incessantly effervescing, ,it prattled and gurgled down over the age old cascade bedrock, to soften and fade out in the shadows of giant trees.

The full moon in a crisp, clear sky formed myriads of shadow designs upon a carpeted glade. There, two fearless young deer leaped logs and shadows as noiselessly as the silent code that passed between them and mother doe, concealed in the deep brush.

Such was the Indian's lost world.

It is difficult at times in the rugged western slopes of the Cascade Range to locate primitive camps. The naturally dense growth of grasses, brush and heavy timber sheds leaves and needles. Trees fall and rot, all forming a mulch covering over camps of long ago. This problem is not experienced in shell mounds; they lie open before your eyes. Caves are confined within their own walls. The barren miles of desert hunting is accomplished by a geographical study of shore irregularity, evidencing the prehistoric, inland sea basin. The extremities of mountain terrain, however, are slower to travel and much harder to carry tools and screens over. Yet, little by little we discover and piece together the Indian life that once existed in the vastness of deep canyons and towering peaks.

Indications are that the cunning, warlike Rogue Tribes and the powerful Klamaths to the east maintained a long period of respect for each other; either through friendship, fear of the other's striking power or simply contentment with their own hunting environment. We see some signs of trading, but as a whole each clung very much to their own designs, traits and cultures. The Rogue's beautiful, long, barbed jasper or agate arrowhead is rare in the Klamath region; while the side notched Klamath point is not too common in the Rogue Basin. A natural overlapping is seen in the high Cascades (more by the Klamaths) but the east-west summits seemed to have been pretty well respected. Most likely, the Klamaths felt secure on their western mountain flank, watching for possible trouble from their suspicious eastern neighbors. As long as the Rogues made no move of aggression, they were content to let things rest.

Mountain artifact hunting is deceptive in the sense that many collectors expect to find a permanent or well established dwelling site. This area is and has long been a special range for big game. Evidence shows that thousands of hunting parties have followed the trails, camping for short periods in some of the most inaccessible places.

They made a few arrowheads or spearheads and possibly a sharp skinning knife. On the ground they left chips and spawls. Broken points were most likely taken from dead game. Builtup firepits don't appear in these layover camps; should one be found, it will be nothing more than an ash stained hole.

Eliminate such places as good lodge sites because of their undesirable locations, water supply and (in later years) their remoteness from pony grazing grounds. This leaves but one course to follow; begin a systematic search for the things not normally found in the hunter's temporary camp. Confine this to a small area.

Figuratively speaking, few full moons have come and gone since moccasins shuffled over the banks we fish from today and willow smoke filtered through out recreation areas. Smoke racks sagged with salmon and jerky, while voices unheard by white man echoed from campfire to campfire across the shadowed playgrounds of the little fellows. A peaceful moon slipped over the western horizon and primitive camps of the Athapascan were at rest. The picture was then one without flaw.

But, as on all Indian frontiers there came that fateful message; the whites were advancing into their northern settlements. Hostile Rogues gathered for battles, which (inconceivable to them) would terminate in the complete destruction of their Rogue Complex. The Great Spirit had spoken over the last council fires. White chiefs filled peace pipes with smelly agreements before starting reservation drives. Regretfully, many isolated events were tainted with misleading reports and filed in saddle bags.

How far wrong was one old survivor when he said, "Why white man all time make bad for Injin? He kill all in Injin camp. He say 'skirmish with hunting party.' Injin fight back for family's lives. He say, 'Injin massacre whites'."

So it is from the cold ashes of camps once warm in the Indian's hereditary land of peace and plenty we attempt to assemble another page from his unwritten diary.

The Monarch Cache

The old scarred spruce tree pictured in Fig. 126 stands out as one of my greatest discoveries. A study of its general appearance and the scars on the top side of its lower limbs led to the caches featured in this chapter. They spoke of decades of skinning game.

My daughter June and her husband, Charlie had run onto a few chips and crude arrowheads here; indicating a camp of some sort on the high divide between the Rogue River and Umpqua River water sheds. They mapped out the route in and I immediately went to look the place over. If it seemed the least bit promising, I planned to dig a number of exploratory holes.

Using the old monarch tree as a focal point, circling trenches were dug, spaced around two feet apart. In the second circle out indications of human habitation became quite pronounced. The appearance of ash, charcoal, and broken animal bones along with a couple of arrowheads speeded up my operation considerably. That protective ridge cupped around the northerly side and an ice cold spring didn't go unnoticed. This was a location little short of perfect for an Indian settlement.

A magnetic trend of attention became centered more and more around the giant spruce tree. This picturesque old timer had a seven foot diameter trunk. It was probably between three and four hundred years old, having withstood fires, lightning strikes and violent winds, losing only some sixty feet of its top. If ever a perfect marker existed from which to cache artifacts, this was it.

Testing long premeditated personal theory, trenching was continued in circles. On the third ring out, about two feet deep, the first group was found. There were ten perfect, heavy, topbarbed arrowheads placed on edge between two square faced rocks with a thin, flat, lidlike cover over them. This special protective attention given them at the time of hiding was a great lead, for it showed their intentions to come back. Strong possibilities now existed that other articles were cached close by. These are simple details, but important ones if the collector is to follow through on faint leads to find what the Indian's plans were.

Ten feet out from the big tree, two to three feet deep, I ran onto one of the most unique finds ever experienced in my collecting career. First, there was a thin, rounded slab of rock four and one half feet in diameter. Upon it, and to one side, was a boxlike buildup of stones like carefully laid bricks. Fig. 127 shows it very clearly. Inside was a cache of 91 small arrowheads, 3/8 to 1/2 inch long (cross type points) and a ceremonial sun disk (Fig. 128). The knife, spearhead and other large pieces were found near the rock slab. The crosses and sun dial seem foreign to this region, showing Central American influence, as did other articles found here later. The tiny points with dainty top barbs were a colorful lot, made from various shades of gem stone; jasper, chalcedony

Fig. 126. Author views giant spruce, badly scarred and minus 60 feet of its top. This old monarch was the monument, or marker used by the author in his trenching pattern. From its base and the surrounding area came the fabulous Monarch Cache. Jackson County, Or.

129

and agate. As one unearths a cache of Indian treasures such as this, all fatigue disappears. You struggle to picture just what transpired in this remote mountainous habitation so long ago.

Possibly these peaceful camps were overrun by another tribe, but considering the time and work to construct these cache sites (particularly those found later) it seems they would need considerable advance warning; which would have been in direct discord to Indian warfare. We might speculate this was trade stock prepared for the Rogues, Umpquas or Klamaths; but from all evidence summed up (after several years exploratory work and findings) we are quite convinced that these people migrated farther along the Cascades. For some inexplicable reason they failed to return and retrieve their valuable possessions.

Operations were suspended that year, but continued at intervals the following summer. Not more than one hundred and twenty feet from our old hub tree another puzzling setup was discovered. About eighteen inches below the surface a long, pointed rock was found, resting on top of four rough mountain run rocks, stacked upon each other. This formed a pyramid going to a depth of about three and one half feet. Fig. 128 shows this unusual buildup. It seemed to have no purpose other than being some sort of a marker. The mixed dirt colors around them definitely revealed it as the work of a human being, as it is impossible to refill a hole with dark top soil and yellowish base soil without leaving a mottled effect in the refill. Using close observation this condition is traceable, and was watched for throughout the diggings here. I puzzled over the five stones in the pyramid. There might be some significance attached to this five feet, five steps, five body lengths. All bore a mystical meaning in Indian measurements and are always worthy of investigation. Half circles and test holes were dug exactly at these lengths from the pyramid. I nursed a hunch it was a guide marker to something important, but winter set in again, ending the digging for another season.

The following year (1957) I renewed the search around the underground pyramid to find I had missed a grooved pestle by a foot, and also found a few ornaments in line with the top pointer rock, out about fifteen feet. This was a very small find to compensate for all the digging done, and though going to camp quite disappointed I knew that old pointer rock was in for another shoveling go around.

My entire family had just arrived at camp to spend the day and have a picnic dinner with me. While eating, though having a wonderful time, my mind was out there searching every avenue. "What haven't I done?" Here was food for thought. "Could it be those Indians were far more shrewd than we had given them credit for? Did they place a few pieces where (if ever discovered) they would distract attention from the main cache?" Just theory of course, but where is the collector who hasn't resorted to some of the most fantastic ideas?

That August day was like the old Indian had said, "Hot like flea under cook's belt " but the boys and I went to work with picks and shovels to either prove or disprove this lingering thought. We started in the opposite direction of our former digging, but in

Figs. 127, 128, 129 and 130. *Above, left:* This 4½ foot diameter firepit slab was struck at a depth of 2½ feet. The rock box was found to contain a cache of 92 pieces. *Right:* This underground buildup of stone, found during test holing, was taken to be a marker indicating a hidden cache. This proved to be true. *Below, left:* Approximately 3 feet down, among tree roots, the first cache was found. A few pieces had been removed, but the balance lay as shown by the author. *Right:* Why shouldn't these fellows smile? They've just removed this cache of 392 pieces. Darrell Greb, Earl Moore and Herb Edwards. Monarch Cache, Jackson County, Or.

line, and off the blunt heel of our problem pointer rock. It soon became evident that Indian cunning had failed, for once at least. We trenched out fifteen feet and suddenly ran onto the telltale signs of spotted yellow and black dirt, indicating something unusual again. Here we found a large cache three feet deep under brush and heavy fir roots. Fig. 129 shows the first pieces removed. Little did we suspect that around three hundred and sixty small, fine arrowheads, carved bone trinkets and various colored stone ornaments were in the small mortars next to come out. We were amazed at the many shapes, intricate designing, workmanship and display of gem stone colors.

In one four-inch mortar (with a larger one turned over it) were one hundred and fifteen small to tiny points. In another (protected the same way) were forty-one bone beads and pendants (Fig. 131) which could be carefully handled after sun drying and spraying with plastic. In the third and fourth mortars, or paint pots, lay two hundred and four small ornaments and ceremonial pieces.

Eight of the bone trinkets have engravings such as lines, rising suns, tepees, mountain tops blowing out, a full sun and other designs. The bone work was near disintegration, and required immediate attention. We lost only four pieces.

This was definitely a carefully premeditated cache of valuables. The Indians were very painstaking, hiding it at this depth and protecting each packed mortar from topside injury. No animal could have stepped into the fine work, nor could a falling tree have crushed them. The whole thing was an elaborate display of primitive ingenuity. Only by a stubborn "never give up" attitude were the rare relics traced to their true location.

Fig. 130 presents a happy bunch of fellows behind the great cache of thirty-two pieces of stone work, among them the six mortars and paint pots that held the many artifacts. The stone head effigy, upper right, with a hornlike projection from the forehead sat in front of the cache, like a sentry guarding the valuables.

Ornaments were serrated on the outside edges for sinew fastenings, and were evidently made long before aborigine contact with white fur companies. No sign of trade beads or trinkets of white origin were found in the entire area. Large roots from forests now rotted away had grown down through the caches; this alone points to a time belonging to the prehistoric.

Population figures in a tribe are roughly estimated by the number of rocked up firepits. Finding but four here, we judged this tribe to be fairly small.

The paint pots suggest the grinding of pigment for body tatooing, or painting arrows, feathers, headbands and the many articles made gaudy with red, yellow and black coloring. This was mixed with bear oil or grease, bone marrow and things of this sort. Buckskin and basket fibre took the stain real well.

I have talked to some of the older Yurok people regarding their chin tatooing. The dark bars were emblems of personal distinction, proudly worn by many elderly women in the Smith River Colony and Yurok of the lower Klamath River settlement. The tatooing is done by cutting and scratching the skin until it is well opened up, with sharp edged

Fig. 131. Bone trinkets were buried in mortar 2½ feet deep. When laid out according to the drilled holes, they seemed to form a necklace. They were preserved with clear acrylic, 1-10. Monarch Cache. Jackson County, Or.

Fig. 132. Author's wife and her partner, the pup, run the first screenings that eventually led to the recovery of over 1300 artifacts. Monarch Cache. Jackson County, Or.

Fig. 133. Bone daggers with wooden handles and other similar relics were saved only by author's method of "instant mud casting." When exposed to air, many disintegrated in minutes. Monarch Cache. Jackson County, Or.

Fig. 134. Excitement ran high when this second cache was found; a ceremonial sun disk and 91 tiny points. The knife, spearheads, etc. were close by. Monarch Cache, Jackson County, Or.

stone chips. Then, a previously mixed salve of charcoal (in this instance) and deer bone marrow was rubbed into the raw abrasions and left to heal over. When the scab peeled off, the little girl's chin indicated she was ready for her place in womanhood. An interesting belief was contained in this rough little piece of surgery; the cutting flakes were chipped from a white rock to insure against infection, white being pure. (See Fig. 4, page 19.)

Reopening a Skyline Site

Mapping a spreadout site may serve you well in later years. Fourteen years after first entering these diggings, the old drawing was brought out again. I had not been thoroughly satisfied about leaving one spot and decided to reopen it. Brush and tree growth had changed the surface, and had it not been for the old map it would have been quite difficult to pinpoint the exact spot. It was summertime, so eight of my family and I went back for a three day camping trip.

There was some axe work to be done on large roots, but after a day of shoveling out my old fill and troweling off the side walls looking for indications of mixed dirt colors, the shovel clinked into some large rocks that shouldn't have been there. As in the past, this aroused interest and the family was called in. The stones were in a boxlike formation, with the usual heavy, flat one over the top. We were sure now that this arrangement was not a happenstance of nature and carefully worked it apart. The stone beads forming a necklace were first to come out, followed by a baked clay bowl containing forty-nine ornaments, punches and arrowheads, no better described than by viewing the pictures (Figs. 137, 138, 139, and 140).

Figs. 137 and 141. inclusive, show extreme ingenuity in workmanship, which perhaps developed from influences far beyond their present horizons. From these excavations clay bowls, sun disks, crosses and unique styling touches may later be identified with a Central American culture. Simultaneously, Columbia River type engravings and skills were recognized. It will require many more years of archaeological findings to determine definitely which link goes where in reconstructing the long chain of human existence.

Many think of the headdress ornaments in Fig. 141 as being beyond the primitive's capacity of styling and fashioning such elaborate body adornment;but at the same time we have accepted the intricate and beautiful designing in primitive basket construction which equally exemplifies their capabilities. These rare discoveries help credit them with skills and achievements we have possibly failed to recognize and respect.

There were no human burials found in this Skyline Site, which does not necessarily disprove there being some in the outside perimeter. If there were deaths here, it is possible the body was disposed of by cremation as it was the early tribal custom in the Klamath and many other regions. Then, too these people could have dwelt here for thirty years or more with little or no loss of life and moved on with their full numbers.

Another widespread burial rite was that of placing the wrapped body in something like a wicker basket and then securing it to a pole frame, or hanging it from tree branches. Columbia River Tribes used the off ground, pole frame burial quite extensively. Many tribes of the Montana Sioux buried in tree baskets, mostly for spiritual appeasement and secondly as protective measure against wild animals.

My wife and I went to a mountain tree where a little Indian girl had once swung from a low branch. We scratched around under the branch with our fingers and found shell beads among glass trade beads, but nothing was left of the remains or burial basket. This was near Ekalaka, Montana.

The absence of any sign of human remains (as in the Folsom Sites) points to the possibility the bodies were left to animal disposal; where the spirit again lived and that animal was either worshipped, respected or feared, complying with the human's attitude in life. The Indian's world, from primitives to the many tribes of today, was strongly influenced by their interpretation of omens from things of nature. Numerous Indian legends, passed down through generation after generation kept alive the belief of powers invested in animal life by their Great Spirit.

Tatoosh, the Thunder Bird, was one of these powers. Because he was so terrible, his picture is painted everywhere in the Indian world. Sometimes he is represented by a single eye. Many Thunder Bird effigies chipped from stone have been found from the eastern states to this western region.

Klamath Indian Creation Legend

*Klamath Indian legend has it that at first **Kaila** (the earth) was flat and bare, but it did not remain so long, for **Kemush**, the Great Spirit soon set to work completing his task. In the valleys he planted grass, camas, iba and iporoots. On **Molaiksi's** steepness he set **Kepa** the pine, **Wako** the white pine and **Ktalo** the juniper. On the rivers and lakes he placed **Weks** the mallard, and **Waiwash** the white goose. **Kemush** put **Mushmush** the white tailed deer, **Ketchkatch** the gray fox and **Wan** the red fox in the forests. On **Ktaiti** (place of rocks) he put **Koil** the mountain sheep and **Lux** the grizzly bear. At last, the world was made. All was new except **Shapashkeni**, the great rock where was built the lodge of the Sun and Moon. Then **Kemush** rolled up balls of mud and shaped them like people. He breathed the breath of life into them and told them to go get wisdom from Wise Coyote.*

So this legend goes, it and many others. Indian legend makes us hesitate to condemn primitive versions of the Great Creation. Being creative by nature their spiritual intuitions and instincts pointed to a beginning of all things. A study of the native's faithful adherence to his spiritual beliefs and inclinations toward mythology helps us to understand the origin of legends arising from the deep, archaic period. However remote they may be these Indian traditions continue to appear in many historical writings; bridges into the past. As such, we are privileged to acknowledge and respect them.

Preserving Bone and Wooden Relics

In 1959, while working behind a good sized firepit about two and one-half feet deep, I uncovered several sharply pointed bone pieces beneath a rotted slab from an old tree. The first one removed was a dagger point with its wooden handle intact, but only a rotted form. It crumbled like ashes within minutes after being exposed to the sun and air. Plastic preservative had been overlooked this trip. How it was needed to save this lot of disintegrating wood and bone relics! Well, when "out in the boondocks," and under emergency pressure such as this, one resorts to some of the most inconceivable methods to save a precious relic. With not even plaster for a cast to hold the bone daggers and wooden handles intact, a desperately conceived, workable solution that proved very efficient was substituted. I went to camp, made a shallow box from a table board, filled it with thin mud and placed the artifacts sideways (about one third submerged) in the substitute mud cast. There the five, eight to sixteen inch bone daggers, hollow lacing needle and other pieces have remained, not a velvet display, yet one that arouses archaeological interest and appreciation for a unique approach to bringing fragile work out (Fig. 133).

Two days later, twenty feet to one side, another fine lot was dug out from under a long, rotted tree section; all running close to the same depth. Fig. 135 shows this discovery cleaned off on one side only, to picture how covered mortars originally lay before being removed.

Number 136 is also part of the lot. Stone effigies of birds and animals, earrings, etc., are pictured separately to better illustrate their real virtues. The animal caricatures leave us wondering just how many they had actually seen, and how many were personal conceptions of ancient legends.

Long Handle and Black Bottom

I was confronted with a time factor during those working years; forced to travel three or four hundred miles; doing my hunting between Friday night and Monday morning, taking the weather as it was. Dragging into camp on burning feet at dusk, my old companions for fifty years "Long Handle" and "Black Bottom " were a welcome sight; soon put to work preparing the evening meal. That old, long-handled fry pan has flipped out enough golden hotcakes to load a pack mule; while the black bottomed coffee pot boils it strong, and pours from a smoked up spout.

Umpqua Murder Unearthed

Fig. 144 shows a chance discovery made on a deer hunting trip in the high mountain water sheds of the South Umpqua, Douglas County, Oregon. While trying to cross a deep water washed gulley I spied a white arrowhead, down about two feet, partially sticking out from the bank. Well, if by this time you are acquainted with me, you know the old rifle was laid aside. With my pocket knife I dug it out and in the process found

Fig. 135. With only one side exposed, this cache was photographed before the mortars were searched. The Indians had covered them with thin slabs of shale rock, for protection. Monarch Cache, Jackson County, Or.

Fig. 136. There is no mistaking a genuine cache. Valuables are grouped in and around such mortars, indicating their intent to return. The Skyline Site is famous for its caches. Monarch Cache, Jackson County, Or.

138

Fig. 137. Stone beads found in 1969 form a beautiful necklace when restrung in order of drilled holes. Monarch Cache. Jackson County, Or.

Figs. 138 and 139. *Above:* Spearhead, knife and clay pot that con-
tained 49 points, punches and headband ornaments in 1969 find.
Below: Exquisite arrowheads and punches for working buckskin.
Monarch Cache. Jackson County, Or.

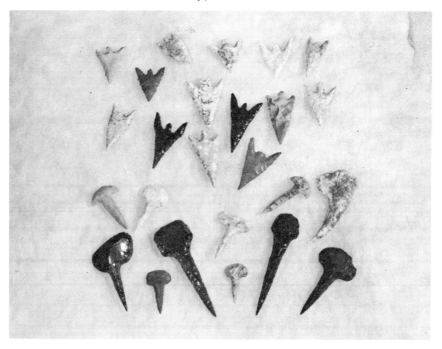

140

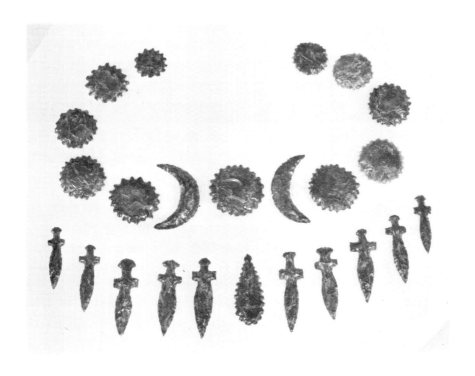

Fig. 140. Dress headbands have always been an integral part of Indian life. These rare bangles and disk ornaments would enhance the appearance of any proud owner. Monarch Cache, Jackson County, Or.

Fig. 141. Intricately designed trinkets of every description, from various colored stones were unearthed in the Monarch Cache. Jackson County, Or.

141

Figs. 142 and 143. *Above:* Stone effigies, chipped from obsidian, jasper and basalt. They were cached in a mortar and protected by a large covering stone. Photo shows actual effigies were chipped from whitish off shades of Jasper. Such stone effigies are very rare. Monarch Cache. Jackson County, Or.

two more. Now the choice between deer and artifact hunting was very easy to make. It only required the time to walk a mile back to the car and trade my gun for a pick, shovel and screen.

As I dug on and on (that day and the next) a sketch was made as work progressed, showing the ground layers, rocked up firepit and the stretched out, face downward position of the human remains. The bones were nearly disintegrated and ashlike, yet traceable, so anyone could see.

The upper right shows a cluster of the largest bone fragments I could gather. The upper left shows the teeth and arrowhead found, just left of the backbone center and under the shoulder blade segments. The teeth had been worn to the gum line, which left little but the roots. A complete set was not found. Whether I missed them in screening, or the old fellow had lost them earlier, I know not. The skull had collapsed and flattened to a jumbled mass, making it difficult to be sure, but the teeth being nearest the underground base was convincing evidence that he had been left face downward. As I removed the cover dirt my shirt and jacket were placed over the bone tracings, so as to not lose the outline and position.

If you would like to try something interesting, lay out some ashes in the form of a skeleton, dampen them down, cover them over with two or three feet of dirt and then try to remove the dirt without losing track of the ash outline, a challenge to the best of archaeologists.

From the best estimate of measurements taken under those conditions this primitive was well over six feet in his youth. There was no piece of the chalky bits of cranium large enough to bring in for age testing so this would be viewed by an anthropologist as an incomplete summary of the discovery; but this one had so very little left for such a study.

This glimpse into yet another Indian's last frontier leaves a few wandering thoughts, paths that may one day merge into the main trail. The findings here tell us little more than that a lone, old, prehistoric hunter (whose well established camp and supply of points indicate he had lived here for some time) was killed by another primitive's arrow. Apparently, he and his possessions were left untouched after he fell face down.

Such discoveries are commonplace when viewed from a lifetime of archaeological explorations. They are recorded in pictures and writings to stand as a part of our history. Through them, more of the previously unknown fits into the pattern, reconstructing the lives and activities of our native Americans.

The primary intent of this book is not to overstress these many great finds, or to inflate the pages with personal involvement in their discovery. The first and most important issue is to impress upon my reading audience the values of following through on even the smallest signs or indications of early human activity. This trend of thought is reminiscent of the giant tree that came from a tiny seed and the million dollar gold mine traced from a few creek colors. So it is with artifact hunting.

Fig. 144. Photo shows how author sketched position
of ancient man, found in washout on the Umpqua
Divide. The insert describes the burial and the artifacts unearthed. Arrowhead *(top, left)* was the murder
weapon, lying in the ashlike ribs. Jackson County, Or.

The Skyline Site has been one of the richest artifact small area fields; and for over
a longer period than most western regions. Hundreds of various surface points were
picked up in the late 1800s and early 1900s. I talked to a very reliable old fellow some
years back, who said as early as 1880, when he came there as a boy with his father on
deer hunting trips with pack horses, arrowheads lay all over the ground. He stated that
not only could they pick up a coat pocket full in a couple of hours, but the dark shades
of gray or black, and slightly blemished ones were flipped aside, just the agate, red, white
and yellow ones were taken along. It is difficult to imagine such a surface display yet our
findings beneath the surface are equally fascinating, and more lie yet, awaiting the persistent hunter in the Skyline Site.

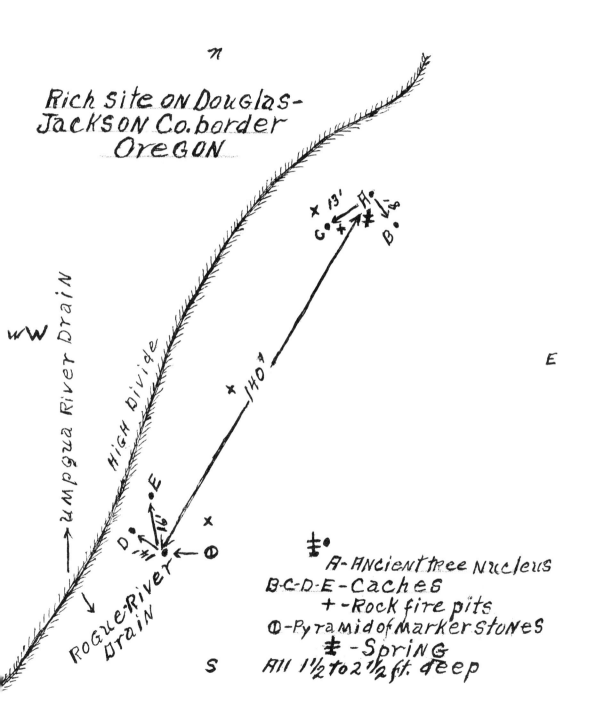

Fig. 145

Rich site on Douglas-
Jackson Co. border
OreGON

n

ww

Umpqua River Drain

High Divide

Rogue River
Drain

+ 140°

x 13'

E

S

A - Ancient tree Nucleus
B-C-D-E - Caches
+ - Rock fire pits
⊕ - Pyramid of marker stones
‡ - Spring
All 1½ to 2½ ft. deep

145

146

Chapter VI
GOLD HILL SITE

CHAPTER VI
GOLD HILL SITE

Findings Witnessed Since 1922

The Gold Hill Site was on the southern side of Rogue River, across from the town of Gold Hill, Jackson County, Oregon; a little westerly of a north-south line from the Gold Hill bridge. A sweeping bend in the river at this point built up an adjacent area of silt, sand and sediment; probably during Pleistocene times, as indicated by archaeological testing.

From pioneer days through the 1920s the site was thought to be nothing more than a surface campground of Indian fishermen. Arrowheads were in abundance for pleasure seekers and hobbyists.

Then a turn of events (explained later) brought other archaeological people to the scene, and the search went deeper and wider under the direction of Dr. L. S. Cressman.

For more than thirty years, as time permitted, I had done intermittent trenching, test holing, screening and surface hunting; making notes of my findings. Then the unexpected happened and all excavations came to a sudden, phenomenal end with the complete destruction of the site. After thousands of years of buildup as a favored location for tribesmen, all went downriver in the never to be forgotten flood of December, 1964. It took man milleniums to build, and a rampaging river but days to destroy.

During the final hours of this famous old site desperate efforts were made to retrieve all artifacts possible from undermined, toppling banks. Skeletons crumpled, as water cut farther into these banks. By hurriedly caving off dirt alongside the burials, many fine artifacts were saved. One who has not seen the onrush of a flood can hardly picture how rapidly and thoroughly the surging water was doing its job.

For instance, one portion of the bank approximately two hundred feet from the summer margin of the river split down through an ancient burial, leaving only the broken ends of the leg bones exposed. Alongside one shoulder a twelve-inch, black obsidian blade was found. Seven elongated, triangular shaped spearheads, two skinning knives and two crude hide fleshing tools lay at the bottom. The top of the burial was approximately five to six feet beneath the original surface. Notes were made later as to the depth and position of the burial, the stones used and the type of workmanship they represented.

From another, similar setting came a fine lot of artifacts; well worth the cold soaking it took to get them. This bank broke at a perpendicular angle, taking the skull and some body structure with it. I had been watching this projection for just such an event, and lost no time when it happened. With my bare hands I squeezed through every square foot of mud at the base, and then scraped down the bank face around the remaining portions of the skeleton. The fast rising water was well above my knees by then —it was high time to get out of there. This primitive burial yielded a large stone axe, several four to seven inch spearheads, arrowheads, a fine pair of atlatl weights, a skinning

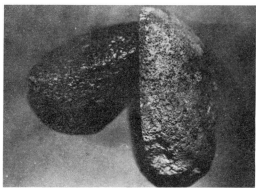
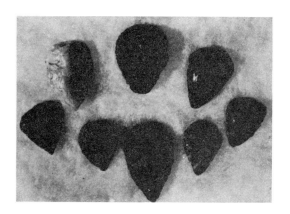
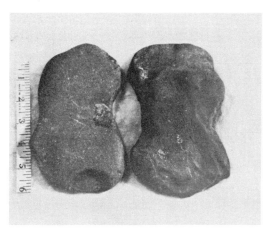

Figs. 144, 145, 146 and 147. *Above, left:* **Skinning knives of the Gold Hill primitive were crude, but served his purpose. Most came from deep down, near bedrock.** *Right:* **Buckskin tanning stones. Hide glue and water were rubbed out, softening the skin while drying. These are 4 to 5 inches long, and show much use.** *Below, left:* **Thumb and finger skin scrapers are concave on bottom, convex on top. These were numerous.** *Right:* **Axes, crude, ill-shaped and battered on edges speak of centuries passed since held by human beings. Gold Hill Site, Or.**

knife and rare artifact known as a slave killer. The burial was again approximately 5 feet below the surface.

In another washed out spot, human bones were detected among the drift and sand accumulation. Work was started as quickly as the water subsided; cleaning out and following bone fragments down to the bottom. A skull and large bones were found that indicated a more recent Indian woman's burial. Debris, sand and gravel were carefully gone over and screened, for we had found a couple of drops (pendants) on the brink of the washout on the previous day. After completing our work, we had thirty-eight jasper and agate neckpiece ornaments, one to one and one-half inches long, grooved around the top end for threading. The elaborate decorative neckpiece no doubt was on her body at the time of burial; for most of the beadlike pendants washed along in close contact with the remains. Now assembled in a glass case, it makes a colorful display.

These last moment findings are mentioned especially to encourage collectors just entering this field of study. Stick with a proven site, as long as there is any evidence of remaining historic value. There might not be another opportunity.

Prior to 1920, kids (now in their senior years) gathered arrowheads to sell to townspeople, gold miners and money spenders in the saloons. In 1931, new developments brought about a wave of community excitement, and first put the Gold Hill Site into the limelight of archaeological interests.

An inevitable but natural public reaction follows each new discovery of Indian artifacts. Invariably, there exists the individual who comes rushing in to "hijack" artifacts. The owner in this case was just the man with plenty of temperament and physique to down a couple of fellows and "repossess" the wrongfully pocketed artifacts.

At this time the property owners were Mr. and Mrs. William Hittle. Neither they nor anyone else suspected the great Indian site that lay beneath the surface they had been farming for years. Surface points had come out with plowings; but no one dreamed of the vast field of primitive burials down to seven feet deep.

It all began when our friend Bill decided to level off a knoll nearly in the center of his field with a team, plow and scraper. Plowing continued for a few days, and dirt was dragged to the low corner, leveling the knoll some three feet. Then, without warning, the plow went through one skull, then another, and then three more. Bill called me to come over and see what I thought about all this. A few hours later, (and before I could get there) he ran into two river boulder type mortars, stubby pestles, a fine metate and several arrowheads; forerunners to the big surprise. The plow then rolled out six long, stone, tubular pipes up to twenty inches in length. These unfamiliar relics were almost too much for Bill. He gathered them into his arms, along with some other fine pieces and went to the house. He entered laughing and said, "I think I dug out an old chief and I'm sure he was a musician. I got a whole mess of his flutes." He was blowing through one, as if expecting to hear musical tones coming forth.

Immediately following this, a number of beautiful obsidian ceremonial blades were discovered, enhancing the findings beyond measure and causing the previously mentioned

150

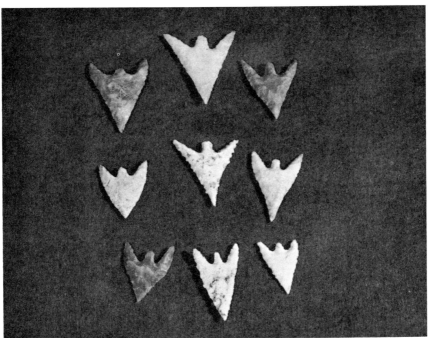

Figs. 148 and 149. *Above:* These Rogue River points are rare. Long top barbs show extreme skill in working jasper and agate. None of these are obsidian. No points are more highly valued. *Below:* Extremely barbed points are identified as slightly pre-history. Gold Hill Site, Or.

151

commotion in the little town of Gold Hill. It was quite comparable to an early day gold strike. The Hittle residence became a very popular place. The University of Oregon was notified, and Dr. L. S. Cressman took charge. The public was excluded from the premises, while operations continued with the team, plow and scraper. The first deep trench revealed things requiring extensive excavations. This became one of the greatest opportunities ever afforded archaeologists in the study of Oregon's tribal dwellings. Varying depths showed continuous occupation back to a prehistoric people, but who could dream how prehistoric?

During the next several months the State working crew unearthed an enormous amount of artifacts. Of course, we didn't know the extent of the findings until Dr. Cressman's bulletin was published, later. As long as the operations continued, I kept a close watch on small areas they bypassed; these I would explore after they left. This netted me several hundred more artifacts.

A most exciting thing at this particular site was an abundance of the rare and famous Rogue River arrowheads. These are known far and wide by collectors, as they are so artistically made, with the long top barbs. The most impressive description of these beauties is accomplished by referring the reader to Figs. 148 and 149. After a thorough study of these prints, I feel positive most will agree, and appreciate these as one of the finest examples of craftsmanship and skill coming out of the Stone Age. Crafted from various shades of yellow and red jasper, obsidian, agate, chert, and chalcedony the points are very colorful and eye catching, in addition to the superb flaking.

Evidently, large chunks of jasper were carried to the site from deposits in the mountains to the east. I have explored these deposits and found where thousands of pieces have been spawled off of jasper boulders; apparently to take back to the campsite. These natives seemingly placed a high value on jasper, for in two burials washed out I found a large chunk in each; one of beautiful colors, roughly eight inches square that would work up into possibly over one hundred fine points.

Six different types of points were found, due primarily to existing layers of habitations; an indication of the intervening periods of time. The ground was formed by layer upon layer of sedimentary river fill in. Evidently ancient tribes moved in upon the new surfaces, for there was clear evidence of evolution taking place in points at varying depths; from bedrock triangular shapes to the extremely barbed top points. This span of time has been estimated at between two and three thousand years.

There was an unusual amount of leaf shapes in the vicinity of the obsidian ceremonial blades; probably an early contact with the hard working jasper stone, yet to be developed into famous barbed arrowheads. There were great numbers of the stubby, punkinseed type or fish points, with little regard to anything other than a rounded, egg-shaped head.

Another item found near the surface bringing forth comment and discussion was the fine long point with a well projected top barb on one side, and a short or entirely missing barb on the opposite side. Though the short one was nearly finished up, the

Figs. 150, 151, 152 and 153. *Above, left:* Heavy triangular spearheads, found near bedrock after the flood, are believed to be the original projectile of the Rogue River aborigine. *Right:* These spearheads show a slimming and lengthening of the triangle, forming a more serviceable spearhead; suggestive of evolution in Indian concepts. *Below, left:* Spearheads showing further change in base, a development probably required for better shafting. *Right:* Leaf shaped arrowhead followed simple ovaloid type at lowest depths. The development of points was easily traced through the various depths of the site. Gold Hill Site, Or.

153

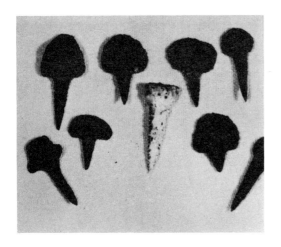
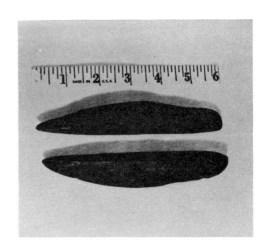

Figs. 154, 155, 156 and 157. *Above, left:* Some 30 punches and drills were found at various depths, showing use of this tool in all past generations. *Right:* Finding of atlatl weights was a real surprise, as no previous link had been found between Rogue River primitives and the atlatl throwers. *Below, left:* Rare obsidian blades and stone pipes, among other artifacts. All are from the 2000 year period. *Right:* Stone implements recovered from the site in 1931. Gold Hill Site, Or.

point appeared somewhat lopsided. It is reasonable to assume that this was the outcome of a stone not working out well on both sides. One barb possibly broke in the making, opening the groove too close to the outside margin. It seems the point, though not perfect, would be as serviceable as any. I hardly agree with some that the minute difference in equal side balance would deflect the arrow, as we find many points with offset heads, heads notched on one side only, thicker on one side than the other, and so on.

Near and on bedrock, crudely hammered out (percussion formed) triangular, and elongated triangular spearheads seemed to all be made of riverrun bedrock. Fig. 150 shows three of several found in bedrock crevices and the adjoining creek bottom. There was no visible sign of flaking depressions on these, only the irregular margins from percussion fractures.

These primitive Rogues (some two thousand years ago) seemed to have not yet developed a knowledge of the fine technique in throwing off paper thin flakes. I did find evidence however, in the deep excavations, of a gradual change coming over points. They were drawn in on the outside of the head end, for better shafting. These deep diggings presented great comparisons; necessary in following the evolutionary changes taking place in arrowhead and spearhead styling and efficiency.

The question arises, why we find this primitive, crude work on the same level or slightly below burials containing large blades of the highest perfection? It would seem plausible to suggest these undeveloped artifacts were made even prior to the large ceremonial blade era. These beautiful blades were brought during migrations into this site, and from all evidence by trail blazers back to the land of the Yuroks on the lower Klamath River. To this day such blades are seen in the White Skin ceremonial dance of these people.

To my knowledge, no other western site has given up as many of these fine specimens. At no time prior to the flood, nor after the field crumpled and washed to bedrock, did we see any large obsidian spawls to confirm their being made here.

A numerical breakdown shows Dr. Cressman's crew with six black obsidian blades, seven red and one slate. We have one red and five black. Other parties have two black ones. These, together with eight freshly broken sections from others (found after the flood) give us an idea of the primitive's possessions. That they were held in high esteem is seen by their burial with the owner.

Ingenuity and skill is recognized in the workmanship on the long, dark slate, tubular pipes. They plainly show circular rotation drill marks and stone chisel cuts, parallel with the pipe, made in removing the core. They were worked from both ends, as shown by the slightly off center hole junction. They have retained the outside polish and, amazingly, four of the six found still held some three inches of charred, fibrous plant material in the bowl end. There was evidence of much smoking in the tooth worn depressions on the mouth end.

Archaeologists agree that the Gold Hill Site was a focal point of four converging territorial influences. This is strengthened by a comparison of styling and designs of stray points found here. Occasional ones on or near the surface showed a definite con-

155

nection with those from adjacent areas; but the Rogues invariably clung to their original patterns. Area comparisons made from numerous outlying camps throughout the Rogue River Basin and surrounding mountains place the central, and possibly oldest habitation at Gold Hill. By the wide distribution of local artifacts we visualize the branching off of many small groups; moving into favorable locations of hunting and fishing. Artifact chips and spawls from stone working are found practically every square mile of southern Oregon westerly from the Cascade summits, to a depth of approximately twenty to fifty airline miles.

Claims to their homeland by right of birth and continuous occupation was bitterly contested, until the end of the Rogue River Indian wars. Military pressure cut them to weakened, roving bands. They have now ceased to exist. Hard hitting cavalry and foot soldiers, (backed by the new portable cannon) along with the help of pioneer volunteers did their job well. We wonder how well, as we review the pages tainted with hatred, revenge and annihilation.

As we lived near and alongside the site for forty-four years, the work continued, and 1961 brought in a new discovery.

We were developing a spring water system on our place west of Kane Creek, between Interstate 5 and the old Gold Hill Site. This required a trench two hundred and twenty feet long and eight feet deep; through half the distance. No artifacts were found during the excavation.

Then, as things happen beyond our control, we found the next morning that a long section of bank had caved in; some four feet back and six feet deep. A crude spearhead was seen protruding from one bank, and this brought the family running. Son-in-law Charley came to help shovel out tons of cave in, and to slope back the dangerously perpendicular bank. We dug into the pocket of fine artifacts shown in Figs. 158 and 159.

The stone, triple holed mortar is the only one I've seen or heard of in my seven decades of collecting. It is pictured from three surface views to miss nothing of its unique design and special side engravings (Figs.158 and 159). The artifact is 6¼ inches high x 5¼ inches wide. We might well accept my old Yurok Indian friend's version of the three holed mortar; thinking it to be used for grinding paint ocher (pigment) or a medicine man's abstract idea of a compound herb grinding mortar. Whatever the intended use, it makes a splendid display artifact, and the margin of almost never knowing it existed makes it doubly appreciated.

Moccasin shaping stones are quite interesting, and found in most well established campsites; though often they are thrown aside by amateurs as just another rock. The moccasin can be stitched to shape over the form, and it was also used to dry wet moccasins. When heated, they retained their shape. One form served for both right and left moccasin by simply turning it over.

The two lower left items in Fig. 159 are implements used in pounding meat, cracking out bone marrow, breaking campfire wood, driving stakes or other endless camp needs. Smooth faced pounders were also used to loosen the glue in hides, to begin the tanning process.

Figs. 158, 159, 160 and 161.　　*Above:* Found on author's place on Kane Creek, 1961, at a depth of 6 feet. Mortar, pestles, wood breakers, moccasin mold and rare triple paint pot. engraved with mythical animal of Indian Gods. *Below, left:* Extremely rare fire carrying pot, found in washout after high water, 1962. *Right:* An 18 inch fleshing tool, found near fire pot. Gold Hill Site, Or.

Digging implements are a simple little tool; with a history back to the beginning of human existence.

The Indian has held to a steadfast respect for the unseen powers invested in his Great Sun. Full sun or rising sun emblems portray their instinctive recognition of a bountiful spiritual hereafter. We are familiar with these emblems; painted on skin tepees, cliff faces, used as body adornment, engraved on bone, stone or shell. I might add that we have two fine, symmetrical, serrated sun emblems fashioned from obsidian; part of an underground cache.

An occasional writer pictures the Indian as a savage, revengeful, a relentless enemy, but excludes the mention of a trusting friend if so approached. Most tribes sensed their inferior wisdom to that of a Great Chief up there somewhere. Sacrifices were made; exhaustive chanting and dancing went on for days, and pain was inflicted upon bodies beyond endurance. We might realize this was done to get through to the spiritual abode above. Therefore, as open minded beings we leave to the sincere Red Man his answering voice in the sun, winds of the forest, thunder rumblings, or from the crags and peaks. It was his interpretation of contact with the hunting Domain of Kemush, the Klamath's Sky Chief; or the happy hunting grounds of the Columbia River's Great Tyhee Sahale.

Fire Carrying Pot

We have one relic seldom heard of, and not seen in most collections. Pictured in Fig. 160 is a fire carrying pot, found after high water of 1962 in the north bank of the Gold Hill Site. The relic was partially exposed, and first thought to be a skull. It was revealed as another rare link in the reconstruction of the lives of our Rogue River primitives. It is 9½ inches in diameter, 6½ inches deep, grooved around outside middle, (four upright grooves) to hold rawhide carrying straps. Indian ingenuity is seen here; this type of volcanic formation was light, and would not break under extreme heat. The pot is well burned on the inside, and still contained charcoal.

Fire was an all important factor in Indian camps. Wet weather often hampered the ignition of materials by stick friction or flint sparks on long travels. So, on these seasonal journeys to mountain berry patches and hunting grounds, a pot of live coals at the end of day was soon the start of a night fire. Throughout the day's march, cones, punk wood or any slow burning material was added, and the coals kept alive.

Years back, an elderly Indian woman from California said she remembered (as a small girl) lugging fire coals along with her people day after day, as they climbed to high mountain country for the summer.

Some used green willow baskets lined with thick mud, but this was heavy and the willow dried, burning if too long in use. Flat shale slabs, with built up mud pits were cumbersome. Pitch torches were of short duration, and other ideas were tried; most of which ended about the second night by the trail side.

We are quite sure we're correct in saying that this fire pot was 100% approved by the Indians who used it; being light to carry, impervious to heat, and roomy enough to

158

hold a half gallon of live coals. As travel continued, night after night, we picture a little flicker beside the trail; the fire pot awaits another day.

Rogue River Indian Foods

The large numbers of specially designed fish points, and large game heads indicate that their main food supply was smoked salmon, deer and elk. A smaller number of so-called "bird points" would indicate water fowl, squirrel, birds and possibly rabbit was only a supplementary source of food.

Heavy stone digging implements tell their own story of the search for bulbs, roots, tubers, sprouts and numerous other ground foods.

The large pumice fire carrying pot, well burned inside and grooved for carrying straps, was evidently used on long trips to the mountains during wild berry season, or similar treks as an assurance of a night fire.

Hide working tools were plentiful on all levels of occupation. These ranged from the little thumbnail fleshers to one sixteen inch, two handled pole grainer and flesher. There were many rounded, flat, smooth faced (one side) rubbing stones, used in drying and softening the tanned hide into velvety buckskin. I have experimented with these seemingly crude stones, and found them to be equal to, or more efficient than steel in tanning.

The devastating flood of 1964 exposed dozens of heavy metates and short, stubby type pestles. This display of weighty stone settled on or near bedrock as the sand and soil was swept away. A reasonable assumption is that most of the mashing and grinding of various dried foods was done by metate, stubby pestles and mano stones, rather than in the few small, boulder type mortars. There was scant evidence of acorn, seed or nut flour being ground at this site; for this would require larger and deeper mortars and longer pestles.

Grinding Implements

Grinding mortars were not as plentiful as one would expect from such a long period of continuous habitation. Small boulder type mortars would eliminate the grinding of acorns and wild seeds for flour, as this requires deeper and larger ones.

We gather from the presence of so many heavy, slightly concave metates that pounded strips of dried and smoked meats constituted the staple food.

From Indian friends we learn that mortars (Fig. 181) with holes in their bottoms, were not always worn out, discarded mortars. They were often used, and are to this day (among scattered tribes) in siphoning off the bitter from acorn flour; by seeping fresh water down through a sand base. Many times a basket was placed inside the mortar and filled with flour, where it was given the same fresh water treatment; the basket retaining the flour. Useless as those open bottoms may seem, that opening was put to a specific use. Some species of roots, herbs and tubers were ground and leached by the same method as acorns.

159

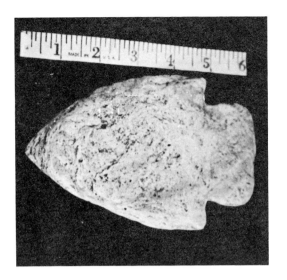

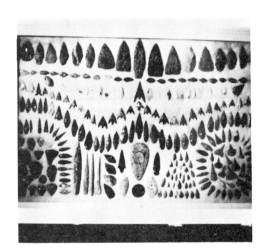

Figs. 162, 163, 164 and 165. *Above, left:* This artifact, believed to be a ceremonial piece, was found in deep underwater crevice at the confluence of Kane Creek and Rogue River, after the flood of 1964. *Right:* One of 9 groups found between 1925 and 1964, before flood. *Below, left:* Cranium, washed out by 1964 flood, acquaints us with early migrant to Rogue River Valley. *Right:* About 1/3 of the points gathered during and after the flood. Most are jasper, a few are agate. Spearheads are typical bedrock, percussion made. Gold Hill Site, Or.

Atlatl Age Contact

Indications are fairly clear that the forerunners of the later Rogue Complex were in contact with the atlatl age. The finding of a pair of atlatl weights, (Fig. 155) in a very deep, washed out burial is proof enough that the weights were in possession of at least one aborigine at the time of burial. The grooved, pointed pieces, thonged onto a spear shaft behind the head, added to the striking force and gave deeper penetration. I was very fortunate in saving this relic from a crumpling bank that in minutes was gone.

Beads and Ornaments

The absence of white man's trade beads, or any other trade material, definitely sets these early migrants apart from other villagers up and down the Rogue, where thousands of faceted, blue trade beads have been found in screening. Without exception, Southern Oregon's historic tribes traded almost any possession for a handful of those big blue beauties, the distribution being noticeably widespread. This fact eliminates contact with the white man, and establishes a major timetable in placing Gold Hill's last Indian habitations. Without question, it verifies the site as being the earliest in this territory.

Native trinkets and body ornaments found here were fashioned from their own familiar and available materials; styled to comply with personal concepts of beauty. Dentalium, olivela shell beads, drilled designs from abalone shell, bone and stone pendants, (two from three to four inches long, engraved with a full sun and a rising sun) drilled bear teeth and stone necklace drops were among the findings in crevices and sand pockets. We are reasonably sure that great quantities of shell and bone decorative pieces washed away with the soil, judging from the many we found trapped in such pockets and from previous excavations.

Sudden Evacuations

An unsolved mystery in the Gold Hill findings is identical to others I have observed in half a dozen well established sites; the undisputed evidence of a sudden evacuation of the site.

Dr. Cressman was the first to detect this in Gold Hill. Quoting from his bulletin, "For example, at site number 9 there were found a number of stone tools, probably women's tools for dressing hides or working up basket material, in perfect order side by side, just where they had been left."

Flood waters could account for quick evacuations on river frontage; but when the exact situation is found in sites far from any water destruction, we then assume the most reasonable cause as being that of sudden enemy raids. In a more recent digging in Lake County, Oregon, I found over twenty bone tools, apparently suddenly abandoned. As in the Gold Hill site, they were in perfect order, side by side, as though the Indian woman had just laid them there the night before. As we visualize the arduous procedure of splitting out, scraping, sanding and polishing these much needed tools, we know the Indian women did not abandon their needles, awls, punches, spacers and basket working tools except through dire necessity.

161

Who Were The Rogue River Indians?

Who were the Rogue River Tribes? Where did they come from? How long ago did they make their first appearance? The summarized bulletin,—"Final Report on the Gold Hill Burial Site," by L. S. Cressman, Ph.D. Professor of Sociology, University of Oregon gives us the answers. For this November, 1933, University of Oregon publication, we are gratefully indebted to Dr. Cressman.

To identify these prehistoric people, we read a paragraph from the summary in this report, quote, "Further, the culture has its focus on the lower Klamath River. The anthropometric evidence suggests a pre-Athapascan group related to the coastal population of British Columbia. The problem of origin and relationship of the Gold Hill people emphasizes the pressing need for archaeological research in Oregon, an area which has hardly been touched," unquote.

Dr. Cressman also stated the Gold Hill burials were prehistoric. The earliest burials go back perhaps two milleniums or more; probably contemporary with the early culture of the Eburne Shell Mound People, on the lower Fraser River.

Summarizing the historic values of the discoveries at the famous Gold Hill Site, we obtain a very complete and living picture of the primitive forerunners of Indian tribes filtering into the Rogue River Valley. The most probable origin, and period of migration has been established by Dr. L. S. Cressman through his seven foot deep exploratory excavations in the sand ridge laid down by Rogue River; probably in Pleistocene times.

Based on a lifetime of field experiences and meaningful observations, I doubt very much if present or near future scientific explorations will be able to compile a more complete record of living activities of the prehistoric Rogue Tribes than that found in the Gold Hill Site, from 1920 to its destruction during the 1964 flood. Artifacts are the work of human hands somewhere, sometime along the millenniums. Regardless of regional variances, depths, abstract designing, (be they crude or highly developed) the message is surely there; if we are capable of interpretation.

This B.C. habitation verified the use of clothing and body ornaments; fashioned from various shell life, stones, drilled animal teeth and bone. We can assume there was a great variety made from perishable materials, such as buckskin, fur trims, grasses, woven work, dyed wrappings, gaudy necklace regalia; and much we know nothing of.

We have noted the highly developed skill in the making of large, black slate, ceremonial pipes. It is amazing to see the work done in drilling out the cores, one of which is over twenty inches in length.

It was the summer following our devastating flood that we abandoned the famous Gold Hill Site. Gravel deposits on fields down stream had been screened, drift packs cleared off to screen below, wild berry vines cut away, and tons of mud and sand were troweled from around the roots. All that was humanly possible to do had been done.

Figs. 166, 167, 168 and 169. *Above, left:* Stone game balls had an important place in early Indian sports. *Right:* Klamath gambling stones. Passed from hand to hand in a game similar to musical chairs, these have won or lost many trinkets, trophies or horses. *Below, left:* Indian workshop. Arrow straighteners, chisels, wedges, axes and sanders. Note rare dugout planer, upper left. *Right:* Mano stones, double handled grinders and most famous kitchen tools, the pestles. Gold Hill Site, Or.

Nude Artifact Hunting

The ceremonial spearhead seen in Fig. 162 will always bring to mind a cold, but invigorating experience. After the high waters receded, I spied this fine specimen at the bottom of a deep hole, just off the Rogue River, in the mouth of Kane Creek. It was January, and the water was ice cold. Enough said, it had to be retrieved.

Using the "old strip" method, I took my clothes off, behind an uprooted tree; gave a quick look across the river toward town, and (seeing no one) made a quick dash over the gravel bar. This being no season for fig leaves, I grabbed an armful of drift brush, (which provided a sort of camouflage) and dove in to my armpits.

I retrieved the artifact alright, but (you are probably ahead of me already) a car did come along. From the heads bobbing at the windows, it would seem they had spotted something over my way; they started to turn around. This was my chance! No time was lost, getting back over that gravel bar. After a good warming up, I prized that relic above many in the collection, and chalked up as successful one of my most farfetched experiences. There was no special news bulletin, that night, warning people of a nude maniac over on the river.

Even though I have over fifteen hundred various artifacts from this location on display, and recorded data in writing, we regretfully recognize the great loss of a wonderful primitive campground. I assure you, the many artifacts and any knowledge I may possess of their origin, will be available to field interests; either through personal viewing of them, or the pages of this book. Our young American boys and girls are very receptive to lectures on Indian affairs, when they can actually see the Stone Age arts and cultures in conjunction with the historic explanations. Many Scout groups come to see our collection, and adults in charge unanimously agree that this combined study-lecture strongly impresses youthful minds. Who knows but what that silent little fellow who looks and listens, seemingly engrossed in his own little world of thoughts, may one day become a specialist in the field of archaeology or anthropology?

Another important thing to be considered (as a result of continued Gold Hill findings) is the confirmation of previous reports published by competent men in the field of archaeology. Not by any measure do we question these; but ofttimes discoveries strengthen the somewhat weaker links in the reconstruction of trails leading back to the aborigine. I know of no other Oregon site that has given more concrete knowledge of so many prehistoric habitations, one upon the other, than has this inconspicuous looking area that became so famous. We know of over seven thousand artifacts taken from this ground.

The Gold Hill Site was an Indian village location quite possibly never to be equalled again, any place, in many outstanding respects. It filled in the gaps of knowledge about artifacts used by the recent Rogue River Tribes, clear back to the original primitive immigrants. Rich in Stone Age work from surface to bedrock, time levels and changing habitations were easily traced, as deeper and more extensive searching progressed.

Chapter VII
FROM HERE AND THERE

FROM HERE AND THERE

This chapter is compiled from findings over many western regions. It is not directly associated with any particular major prehistoric site. Yet, it presents various interesting facts necessary to complete any writing on Indian crafts. Photographs and explanations will illustrate the merging of ancient cultures into those of our early historic and modern day Indian societies.

From our previous study of Stone Age artifacts we found that every unfamiliar, odd shaped, finished stone was made for a specific purpose in the Indian camp. Through information passed to us by older tribal members, the relic in question becomes an important implement. I have conversed with many early day Modoc and Klamath friends pertaining to early Indian history. Their willing answers were later found to be very accurate, and right to the point.

Things seen and heard from the living add special significance to the many overlooked articles of sport; such as the stone game ball, gambling stones, bone and sinew buzzers, stone donut hoop and pole tossing rings. Countless numbers of other gadgets were used in games of skill and amusement. The wild Indian was by nature very receptive to sports, games, physical contests, fun and festivities; and so devised many simple, but wildly exciting outlets for pastime competition.

Stone Age Ball Game

For instance, the common stone game ball put betting groups into a hilarious mood as contestants prepared for the rolling event. *An old Modoc, upon seeing one of these balls on our ranch porch, picked it up and smiled. Dad said, "John is that some kind of an old Indian rock?"*

John answered, "Oh yes, he make big fun!" He went on to explain the game.

This was in 1903, and the old fellow had weathered out many confusing years. He had once had his own lodge, and lots of horses, "Long before a big war someplace, where white men killed other white men." The Civil War?

We appreciate his efforts in relating the game.

He said, "One Injin stand by hole in ground here. Other Injin stand by his hole in ground some steps over there," and he tossed a pebble out about fifteen feet.

He continued, "You get now, this Injin roll rock to other hole, and if he go in, no body get a count. But, if other Injin make big powwow, and spirits make ball miss the hole, he get the count."

Now this required some figuring out, but the idea was; when the stone rolled across the sod into the opposite hole it did not score a point for the one who delivered it. It did not score at all. If the one standing by the hole as it rolled toward him could whip up enough big medicine (through all sorts of wild motions and threats to his opponent's ball, to cause a miss) then he scored the point.

So this was the little stone ball game that fired young and old alike into a friendly state of frenzy.

In our search for Indian history we often miss many sidelights in their home life; things that help portray their true and natural characteristics.

Gambling Stones

Elongated oval stones, (Fig. 167) were gambling stones.

I asked an old Klamath how they gambled with them. He said, "Big ring of Indians go 'round and 'round, singin' song talk. You have rock, then you don't have rock. Lots of hands to vamoose in. Pretty soon, everybody stop and somebody got no hoss left!" I told him that I didn't quite understand how the betting was done. His only answer was, "Huh, you easy. You lose hoss for sure!"

It is an astounding sight to look upon a few remaining Redwood stumps on the slopes of the Pacific showing stone axe marks where oceangoing boats have been chopped and burned from the giant trees.

The round stones with a hole in the center (Fig. 167) are classed as arrow straighteners. If there should be a kink or bend, especially in a small limb or twig shaft, it could be removed by working the shaft down through the hole as far as the bend, where pressure was applied by laying a heavy rock across the tilted straightener stone. If it was a bad bend, or in seasoned wood, it was kept wet and given more time to reshape.

The relic shown, (upper left, Fig. 168) is a real novelty among the findings of Stone Age works. Its unique design stamps it as a purposeful, unusual implement. Eliminating all impractical uses, we have accepted it as being a charcoal planer, or plow to gouge out the burned interior of a log during canoe construction. Three lava canoe anchors were also found close by. The eight inch long plane is made with a sharp shaving edge on one end, has a rounded hand grip for the right hand on the other, with a lower grooving to fit the left thumb; a real neat little tool.

Clubs and Tomahawks

The long handled relic in Fig. 173 (from the Sioux country) is typical of those used in killing wounded buffalo, in buffalo"jumps." The Sioux and Cheyenne made great use of these grooved, egg shaped stone heads in the plains of Montana and the Dakotas. Rawhide is placed around the stone while wet or green, then sewn together full length over a wooden handle. After this rawhide dries and sets, nothing is going to move it. Rawhide lacings come from the untanned hide after the hair has been removed, while it still retains the natural glue. It is one of the toughest materials known.

The tomahawk, complete with handle, (next below in same picture) is from the buffalo country, also. The unique handle accounts for its rarity. It is the large tendon from a buffalo's leg, split in one end long enough to force stone through, while yet pliable. The tendon has been held straight until dry and set, making a handle as efficient

167

Figs. 170, 171, 172 and 173. *Above, left:* Stone wind chimes (tinklers) dangled from hooplike branch, amusing papoose. *Right:* The Nau-Ausk (cradle) links yesterday and today's Yurok Indians. Mrs. Nellie Griffin, a Yurok, made and presented this token of friendship to author and wife, when she was nearly 100 years old. *Below, left:* Process from large obsidian chunk to finished blades. It is spawled on the curve, making the artifact thick in the middle, with cutting edges. *Right:* Tomahawk and axe blades played important roles in Indian existence.

Figs. 174, 175, 176 and 177. *Above, left:* Stone image; face with horned forehead, dug out on the Umpqua Divide. It leans heavily toward Columbia River designs. *Right:* Granddaddy oak, estimated to be 1000 years old. It stands 96 feet tall, with a diameter of 9 feet, for 8 feet above the ground. A living monument to Mechoopda history in the acorn region. Chico, Ca. *Below, left:* Moccasin mold, metate, game balls and grooved head. Butte County, Ca. *Right:* Smallest and largest perfect mortars from Chico, Ca.

and possibly longer lived than wood. These items are the finished outcome of Indian ingenuity in fashioning his needs from the rocks of his earth, achievements to be considered.

White Man's Beads

For a diversion from the more strenuous field exploits, screening for beads does nicely, and the findings add a colorful touch to any collection. I have over three thousand various types of shell, bone and stone beads from old primitive sites, and numerous kinds of white man trade beads; including the big blue, faceted Hudson Bay traders.

The initial traders and trappers soon detected the Indian's craving for colorful beads, and realized their own advantage by possessing them. They drove hard bargains in a trade; a mere handful being good for a fine bundle of prime furs. The wise trader called the big blue beauties "Chief's Beads," which again aroused in tribal chieftains a sense of personal distinction regardless of the true value attached.

A question arises here, when picturing the scene of eager tribesmen gathered around the trading circle. Why didn't the Indians kill the few white traders and simply take the coveted beads? No doubt a string of saddle and pack horses stood close by; and even though they well knew that large bags of beads were in those packs, they seemed to respect the rights of personal possession. They chose to trade value for value, rather than resort to savage thievery. In a few short years, however, this trusting attitude was badly shattered, as white aggression prodded the Indian into fits of despair, hatred and revengeful retaliation.

Another factor that tightened trade bargaining from the 1830s on into the 1860s was the Indian's keen instinct, detecting that they were being exploited by white men no greater than they. A line from one of Arthur Woodward's writings clearly expresses the impact of this changing attitude toward white traders, quoting, "It was when the Indians learned that these newcomers were only human, like themselves, and that they valued the furs of the animals which roamed the forests, the mountains and the sea more than they did the objects of metal and cloth, and the glittering baubles of brass, silver and glass, that the aborigines began to strike harder bargains," unquote.

For an interesting and educational study of trade good materials, original manufactures, types and special construction designing, etc., the No. 2, 1965 publication of Indian Trade Goods, by the Oregon Archaeological Society (from the Arthur Woodward series) is highly recommended. Mr. Arthur Woodward is recognized nationwide as an authority on Indian Frontier trade goods.

Prior to the white newcomers with supplies of gaudy objects, Indians were evidently just as enthused over swapping and bargaining for decorative ornaments with other tribes. Though not as showy and gleamy as glass and metal, theirs from the earth and sea represented a greater scope of human ingenuity in fashioning from nature the desired adornment; pearllike abalone and mussel beads and engraved bone trinkets attest to their eye catching beauty.

The drilled and polished stone beads seen in Fig. 192 is another example of the primitive's capability of turning the roughage of nature into attractive ornaments. There are forty-six of these many colored, oblong, rounded and disk shapes, making a re-strung length of two feet.

We might hesitate a moment to consider the time and patience required to drill, with other stone, the twenty-four inches of holes. I cannot conscientiously agree with the few historians who refer to those ancient people as shiftless, uncivilized tribesmen. How truly "advanced" is the modern enthusiast who requires the aid of an electric drill, chisel, sander and stone cutting tools to duplicate the same artistic work?

Time and Effort Brings Rewards

The time and effort spent in the finding of the stone beads was quite comparable to that experienced at Yuba City, California, where undermined river banks had crump-led and scattered artifacts from their original clusters. These in Fig. 192 were screened from the west bank of the Rogue River, up stream two miles from Gold Hill, Oregon. After screening a few from the disturbed dirt toward the river, it soon became evident that the mass of dirt had caved off from the remaining bank. Leisure hours for days were spent in going through tons of bank dirt, and an occasional bead was found somewhat in a line that led to the main lot. These bank tracings from a small lead often pay off, and should be taken note of.

For instance, a good find from a bank on Kane Creek, Jackson County, Oregon came about by spotting a stone axe next to the bank, at bedrock level. A similar one came from a wind blowout face in Fort Rock Valley, where a spearhead was protruding from the face. Five rust eaten, steel spearheads and a copper bracelet (made by white man) were found simply by investigating a rust stain showing down the bank face. There-fore, following through on the least probable lead, though seemingly unimportant on the surface, has often developed into a substantial reward.

Conscience versus Artifact Hunting

Within the range of years spent collecting, one is occasionally confronted with a most unusual and difficult situation. In 1959, on a sultry California day, I was sitting on a park bench watching a bulldozer cleaning brush and debris from the creek channel. A broken pestle rolled out, and to be sure I mentally marked that spot for future inves-tigation. This was Maidu country, and a few Mechoopda tribal relics would find a wel-come place in my collection. It was not by chance that a pick and shovel were in my car, and a small exploration was soon underway. It seemed no longer than thirty minutes before six fine, grooved stone club heads were uncovered.

Simultaneously, there appeared a big fellow whose authority well matched his own bulky physique. He looked down and snapped, "Hey, you, what's goin' on here?"

"Prospecting," says I, while sitting on a half a dozen artifacts.

171

There was no misunderstanding his intent to break up my little project when he said, "You may not know it, but you are still within the town limits. You make tracks farther up the creek to do your 'prospectin'!"

With a "thank you, sir," the hole was reluctantly filled in (after four more fine heads were troweled out).

A strong argument then ensued between myself and I in regard to pursuing this interesting find. In compliance with better judgment (under existing conditions) field etiquette was respected. I left with no regrets, however, having come into possession of the ten primitive artifacts. They fell into appreciative hands for archaeological viewing and study.

Four of the heads were designed for handles to be secured by rawhide wrappings pulled tightly into the groove. The ball-like, smooth ones were evidently intended to be encased in rawhide with rawhide wrapped handles. We have seen both of these separately designed heads (with different methods of securing handles) in museum displays; but we continue to marvel at the aborigine's natural knowledge of rawhide and with what efficiency he put it to use.

With all regard to field etiquette, there are moments of indecision as experienced above when the old maxim "a bird in hand is worth two in the bush," seems to justify the action.

Keep Good Squaw

An old Indian at Bly, Oregon once explained this situation very nicely, though I doubt he had ever heard the "bird in bush" expression. I had just asked him if he traded for his wife.

Suddenly, the answer came. "When you run down good squaw woman, better keep for sure. Maybe next time, wind not so good and you lose all, maybe."

Ancient Water Trap

It was up in the outcropping lava formations, northeast of Chico, that a most interesting thing developed from nothing more than a rest period. While stretched out in the shade of a willow clump, my attention became fixed on something almost at my feet that seemed worth investigating.

That watertight hole, some two feet deep (by the same diameter) up a ways from the dry creek bed on the fairly smooth lava slope, took on the semblance of a little water well; and more so by the several shallow trenches or channels feeding into it. The trenches were about an inch wide, and definitely showed they had been pounded out. After dirt and decay was scraped out, one could follow the trenching up the lava faced incline. It then became evident that this primitive project was constructed for a water trap. The shallow drains led from one small hole to another; but all the time led down to the deeper well.

This little network could have no other purpose that I could visualize. It was a

172

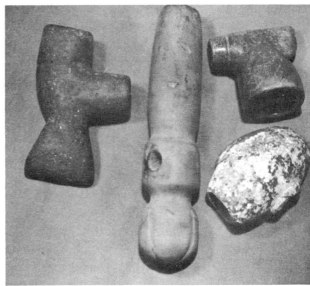

Figs. 178, 179, 180 and 181. *Above, left:* Crevices in the high lava country east of Chico, Ca. still offer overlooked artifacts, such as this metate and mano stone author found in 1960. *Right:* Stone pipes from Douglas, Jackson and Klamath Counties. These are the types seen with long, decorated stems. *Below, left:* Lu-mon, or eel trap, used by Yurok Indians. It is highly prized by us for the friendship that came with the gift. *Right:* Open bottom mortars, used to leach bitter foods, such as acorn flour.

clever system to trap runoff water for camp use. The much needed water could be caught from drizzles or from thunderstorms in dry seasons, and with a brush cover over the new water supply, it would be kept cool and drinkable for long periods after the runoff. Many strange things have to be resolved strictly from a conjectural basis; from a lengthy study of this unique setting, I am convinced that the final conclusion is correct.

The metate and sanding stone (Fig. 178) were found on the opposite bank in a rough lava formation, where they had tipped or washed over into a deep crevice.

The Hooker Oak

The famous old Hooker Oak, seen in Fig. 175, estimated to be over one thousand years old, stands in Chico, California. Ten years back, this giant oak tree stood ninety-six feet tall, had a limb circumference of four hundred and eighty-one feet, with one limb one hundred and eleven feet long. A nine foot diameter oak up to eight feet from the ground is something to see.

We can only speculate how many Indians of past centuries have squatted around this oak of all oaks grinding acorns for flour, and living unmolested lives.

Cradle Wind Chimes

Another, (mostly unfamiliar article) is the papoose cradle tinklers, or wind chimes; an Indian mother's ingenious idea to pacify her babe. They are made from two to three inch long, thin rock spawls; notched at the top, with a tapered end for sinew fasteners, and are slightly curved for a louder tone effect. Wind movement clinks these together, making a soft, musical lullaby that fascinated and entertained the little papoose.

I found eight of these wind chimes in a cluster that had been placed in the side of an old tepee dugout, alongside several stone awls. Fig. 170 illustrates the wind chimes very nicely. I ascertained (from the older Indians) they were not extensively used in western tribes; though I have read in three accounts that pioneers traveling west made friends with tribes along the Columbia, where the "breeze music makers" were seen and heard in front of papoose cradles. My finding of the eight mentioned bears out their being used in that windy area, also. The sound is comparable to that of the glass chimes we pick up at novelty shelves, today.

What did the Indians call the papoose cradle? The name usually varies with the tribe; such as *nau-ausk* by the Yurok people, *te-kash* is heard among the Umatilla, *skene* up around Celilo Falls by the Wy-am-pum (people of the water echoing against the rocks). In the Karuk dialect, we hear *sock-too-ee*. The Klamath mother calls it her papoose's *swentze.*

Sketches and Notekeeping

Notes made and kept from things related by early Indian friends of Klamath and Lake Counties fit nicely into the realistic pattern, as artifacts came from this site. As some of us enter the later years of Stone Age collecting, we learn to appreciate these old filed away notes for the support they furnish in making a correct identification of an unfamiliar object. They are reviewed and studied frequently while working a site such as this one, useful over a period of many years. Sketches were made whenever the camera wasn't handy. (See Fig. 144.)

In the interest of those who may sometime be confronted with the same conditions, but are too inexperienced to realize the great opportunity before them, I impart the knowledge gained through past experiences, along with a bit of advice; do the same.

Smoking Pipes

The stone pipe display in Fig. 179 is from Oregon discoveries. Top left, the old lower Klamath Lake region; top right, Rogue River bank; center and lower right, Skyline Site, Umpqua Divide. Smoking pipes, segments or whole ones, are found in most major habitation sites, suggesting a social pastime pleasure as well as the native's binding seal to unwritten issues in council.

The absence of pipes in some sites seems to verify statements by pioneer writers that smoking was not general in poor, or wandering small tribes.

The first white men to contact western Indians were confronted with immediate decisions as the pipe was passed from the hands of the chief. To smoke was a bid to peace. To refuse aroused suspicion and trouble. This silent, meaningful ceremony was of short duration; but the seal to an understanding lived up to by the Indian. In the following years, however, the white man's volume of versatile words confused the natives; requiring long periods of claims, counterclaims, bickering and government force to execute the same simple agreements.

The bowl type pipes shown were to be used with long stems, as we've seen in old pictures of past Indian council gatherings. Hollow reed stems, wood, fabricated bone and wood and other stem materials were decorated with beads, feathers, buckskin fringe and various showy ornaments.

The Slave Killer

The artifact in Fig. 7 is classified as a slave killer. A color photo of it is shown on page 31. It is a controversial artifact, clinging closely to the same outline throughout the region, and is consistently constructed from blackish slate stone. I have heard many theories and stated facts (supposedly) advanced by archaeologists as to the origin and purpose of the old relic. If any are near correct, then the black animal effigy was a feared killer in the slave camp. Personally, I recall many implements around the Indian camp that would be much more appropriate to give the poor slave his permanent anesthetic.

I have talked with aged Indians about this artifact, but came up with little. However, one old Yurok thought it was a special emblem of authority; similar to that invested in a modern day police badge. It was carried by the one honored with the task of killing captured enemy slaves who were no longer useful. Occasionally, one has notches on the back; which suggests a primitive prelude to the western gunman's notching of his weapon.

175

Figs. 182, 183, 184 and 185. *Above, left*: Stone necklaces, found in 1969 Monarch Cache. *Right*: **Mrs. Moore painted this giant spruce that led to the discovery of the Monarch Cache.** *Below, left*: **Three of the beautiful ceremonial blades unearthed at the Gold Hill Site.** *Right*: **Petroglyphs. Ancient artists recorded important incidents and their culture for the future ages.**

Eel Traps

The *lum-mon* (eel trap) pictured in Fig. 180 was used by Yurok Indians on the lower Klamath River, Northern California. It is made of sturdy limbs and roots, for the load of eels *ka-win* is heavy at times; often up to seventy or eighty eels. If no *ka-win* run, our old friend Seeley says, *"Mus-koos-key-ah-saun,"* (can't do anything about it).

The trap is set in a fast riffle, with small poles about seven feet long driven down as wings in three or four feet of water. Enough rocks are put in the trap to hold it down, and the set is made. Eels working upstream slide along the pole wings and maneuver into the *lum-mon* cone where they are trapped. The trap is examined twice a day if the run is heavy.

Smoked eel is very good, and rates approval when freshly cooked. The little papoose wasn't long in learning to gumsuck a piece of smoke cured eel meat.

Stone Fish Hooks

Stone fish hooks became more interesting after I had occasion to talk with Indian friends about their purpose and efficiency. These were not exempt from breakage, (like our steel hooks), and the Indian was required to use more skill and a different technique in landing the big fish.

The fish was given time to swallow the meat covered stone hook, and was then followed or towed with a fairly loose line to where it could be maneuvered into shallow water; then shot with an arrow, or speared.

These little stone hooks stand more pull than I at first realized. I have hung many weights on one (up to twelve pounds) before deciding to stretch my luck no further. The ten previously seen in Fig. 49 came from a cave in central Oregon.

Spiritual Observances

Numerous artifacts revealed the spiritual realm those primitive Rogue Tribes turned to in council, for good or bad omens, interpreted from the winds, clouds, drought periods, animals, birds, fire, charms, visions, intuitions, etc. We can easily understand such tribal beliefs as an instinctive recognition of a supernatural power; probably in the abode of the sun. Among our artifacts depicting this trend is the flaked out stone sun emblem, the rising sun engraved on the triple mortar side, a full sun engraved on slate pendant, a fine engraving of the rising sun on a large bone pendant and others, all reflecting a reverence toward the sun.

The nationally known Rogue River arrowheads, with needle point, long slender, top barbs, symmetrically flaked from the beautiful colors of jasper stone, apparently originated here on the banks of the Rogue River. They are the envy of any collector.

The summary of my personal findings of forty years at the site answers many requests for information on the B.C. Rogue River primitives. With the gracious, strengthening background of Dr. L. S. Cressman's complete and exceptionally well documented report, (on his 1931 and 1932 findings) it will hopefully lend the reader a better understanding of those prehistoric, migratory humans we now call Indians.

Sand Bread

Hot rock bread (often referred to as sand bread) constituted the main flour-mixed food in acorn regions, or lake wokas areas. Older Yurok people term these hotrock patties *"paupf-paupf,"* and along with *ie-pooie,* smoked salmon or *poo-ook-wa-chel,* dried deer meat, the meal was surprisingly palatable, and very nourishing. These meats were also ground to a fineness, and stirred into a mortar with hot *paa-ock,* water, making a tasty, thickened soup or broth. Much grinding and pounding was required to reduce dried meats to a fine powder base in the making of *Pem-ih-kan.* To this meat powder was added hot fats, and if by good fortune dried berries or fruits were on hand, they were also added. For a convenient travel pack, tallow could be melted in for firmness. The *Pem-ih-kan* mixture was then cut into small cakes. A bag of these cakes would keep the hunter, or whoever, in top condition for many days. With a thought or two to a few of the many important uses of the pestle and mano stone, their value is easily understood.

Basketry

At present we are seeing a noticeable decline in the making of beautiful Indian woven baskets; an art from ancient times to the present day. It is indeed regrettable that this fine craft is fast dying out among our western Indian people; a part of their grand heritage. Sadly, great numbers of the younger people have either forgotten, (or possibly, never learned) how to process the materials required in the making of those world famous baskets.

Willow and hazel branches and roots have lost their value to many. Baking and mashing out threadlike strands from bull pine roots was a procedure once watched with youthful interest. The two flat, tough strands taken from sword fern stalks (after being stripped of leaves and crushed) were things of grandmother's time.

Seldom is a young woman seen making basket trim dye from alder tree bark chips soaked in water; a permanent, reddish-brown color. Black maidenhair fern stalks mashed flat and separated into strips gave another color trim effect to the basket, as did the white blades of bunch grass give color contrast in patterns, design and trim. These blades were extensively used in binding edges and wrapping handles (such as the baby cradle). Most materials used in fine basket weaving were kept soft and pliable by working it while wet.

Allowing for an occasional slight deviation, the design on a basket will usually identify the tribal origin, as they cling to traditional patterns. For example, the California Yokut basketry is recognized by figures holding hands, as if in friendship, with a center band of rattlesnake design. Northwest California Yuroks use the parallelograms, triangles and diagonal trapezoids. The Pomo basket is really flashy, being overlaid with feathers; usually red around the rim and finished around the collar with feathers and beads.

The designs are woven in, stained, or applied to the foundation surface in contrasting shades of red, black, yellow and tones of brown; giving a sharp effect to the finished basket. Thus, throughout the tribal regions we find various and interesting basket designs, conforming to the individual tribe's own hereditary traditions. We may rest assured that whoever originated this great art, it was embodied with love and devotion toward a beautifully expressive outlet.

It has been a gratifying experience to know and be friend to such fine basket makers as Nellie Griffin, Frances Jaynes, Rosie McDonald, Nellie Mays and others from the lower Klamath and Smith River settlements.

Mrs. Nellie Griffin is past one hundred and six years at the time of this writing, and is still making baskets and weaving rugs; a most amazing and congenial Indian lady of the true Yurok blood. We owe so much, and can give nothing but thanks, to the Indian women who have so generously contributed to the fine arts of the world. A personal word in recognition of their rare talent is most invariably answered with a meaningful smile.

Stone Idol

The stone relic viewed in Figure 6 was found in a deep excavation in northwest Oregon, and evidently was not made by Indians of this region. The image has an Oriental bearing that meets with opposition among archaeology scholars. It has been the subject of many debates before sufficient evidence was found to settle on the most probable time and place of its origin.

After a thorough examination, scientific people are of the opinion that it is from an early Aztec culture of perhaps four or five hundred B.C. An early day trading ship may have picked up the idol, (which we believe it is) as a trade item with far north tribesmen. We will never know.

The hands are in a deity pose with six fingers each. Seven toes are on the feet, and body characteristics strongly suggest pagan worship of human-animal idols and statues of fantasy.

This ten inch high figure is apparently shaped from a black volcanic stone, with a thin layer of dark, claylike material fused to the stone surface. Aging or former polishing was instrumental in leaving the smooth surface finish. Whatever its history, it is an odd artifact to be found in this northwest region. In research; we call it the little "sneaker" that seldom comes our way.

Pottery

The pottery field is extensive, and it has not been my good fortune to have been able to explore the southwest for this great art. I can show however, in Fig. 193, what can be accomplished in the way of reconstructing and preserving the ofttimes conglomeration of broken pieces cached away as valueless; the owner holding to the wish that they could be reassembled into a near likeness of the original.

I was quite successful in going through a large box of broken pieces, donated by a family who had many years ago found them in burials behind the walls of cliff dwellings in the Mesa Verde area. Over two hundred pieces were found, showing the same pattern

Figs. 186, 187, 188 and 189. *Above, left:* Willow and hazel brush fruit basket and tray. Woven by Mrs. Mandy McCallister. Right: Large Klamath basket, tightly woven from fern and grass, making an unusually pliable, special work of art. *Below, left:* Lower Klamath River baskets. Parallelograms, trapezoids and triangles in diagonals and chevrons identify Hupa-Yurok basketry, N. W. California. *Right:* Upper Klamath River baskets and tray. Tray shows intermingling of patterns between Upper and Lower River people.

Figs. 190, 191, 192, and 193. *Above, left:* Two of six fine Lower Klamath baskets, presented to us by Nellie George, of Montague, Ca. Alder bark dye, dark fern and grasses are woven in, to form designs. *Right:* Basket type head caps. Hupa-Yurok women made and wore them as part of their heritage. *Lower, left:* Choice lot of stone beads, 1/3 actual size. Dug out above Gold Hill, Or. along the Rogue River. *Right:* Painted pottery, nearly 1200 years old; from cliff dwellers of Colorado and Arizona. The amazing paint of the Anasazi culture remains undimmed throughout the ages.

design, from which I assembled a water jug. By the same method, the bottom bowl in Fig. 193 with inside and outside painted designs, was assembled from over sixty pieces. The work is not easily accomplished; but by such efforts many works of ancient people are saved.

The main obstacle lies in not knowing whether the pieces were from a bowl, platter or jug. Reconstruction necessarily starts with the right angles, to conform to the original shape. It is tedious and time consuming, but very interesting to see the original taking form once again.

This Anasazi culture is referred to by the Navajos as "The Ancient Ones," a culture existing in the period of 1000 to 1200 A.D. It is amazing how the pottery has retained the black paint designs over the years. There is evidence of various forms of the Anasazi culture extending back to 100 A.D. So, when screening, it is advisable to lay aside all pieces. If reassembled, they hold the same historic value; possibly more so.

Sweat Pits

An important factor in reconstructing the Rogue Indian's primitive past came to my attention in 1962. Heavy equipment was leveling off high ground in a field belonging to Mr. Von der Hellen, on lower Bear Creek, Jackson County, Oregon. An operator on one machine, (son-in-law Charlie) phoned me, saying they had come upon several orange colored rings about three to four feet in diameter, some four feet below the original surface.

I went immediately with a pick and shovel, and (with permission) started digging one out. The yellowish-orange rings continued down to five and six feet, forming what had evidently been sweat pits. The absence of ashes and charcoal in the bottoms clearly eliminated their being bakepits.

Clay linings had been patted onto the dirt walls, as hand prints showed, then baked to a bricklike hardness two to three inches thick. The orange colored walls and bottom had fused into the black dirt, presenting an interesting and colorful sight.

By the absence of clay deposits near the sweatbath constructions, it was quite evident that the lining clay was carried a long distance; which in itself was enough to put any sound Indian's back in condition for a "sweatout."

Each pit was filled within a foot of the top with large rocks, blackened somewhat from open fire heating.. As these were rolled or tossed in, most had cracked or spawled off when contacting water. Dirt had seeped in over the thousands of years, leaving the interior a solid pack. Each boulder had to be picked loose; and under a 106 degree sun. Figs. 194 and 195 show two of the seven pits, with walls partially cleaned off for better examination.

There was a large, smooth metate in the bottom of each (possibly of spiritual implication) which was before excavation nearly ten feet deep.

After a thorough study of these sweatbath wells, I was convinced that one could to this day pour in some water, toss in hot rocks to generate steam, and with a skin top cover still heat up an Indian for his cold water plunge; which guaranteed either a quick

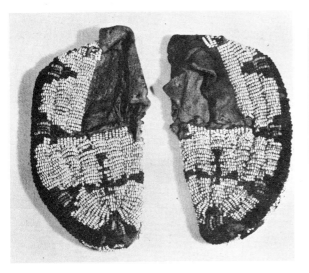
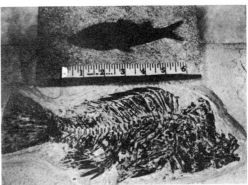

Figs. 194, 195, 196 and 197. *Above, left:* Sweat bath well. One of seven excavated in 1962 along Bear Creek, Jackson County, Or. *Right:* Heating rocks brought up from depth of 5 to 6 feet. They were 3 feet in diameter. Clay linings were patted on, and baked watertight, forming serviceable bathpits. *Below, left:* Idaho moccasins trace back to Civil War days. They show overlapping period, when Indians used trade beads, yet retained sinew in construction. *Right:* Green River, Wyoming, fossilized fish, estimated to be 40,000,000 years old. Labeled by D. C. Haddenham. Period, Eocene. Genus, Knightia. Specie, Alta.

183

recovery or a lingering death. Anyway, we are obliged to give those primitive people credit for their inventive skill and knowledge of firing the clay to a brickhard, water-tight lining.

There were no signs of clay pottery or pipes being made here, nor was any evidence seen of burials. Broken mortars, metates, pestles and hide fleshers were occasionally rolled out. The odds are against one watching the dirt ahead of a bulldozer blade.

We are quite familiar with the historic Indian's treatment of the ill by steaming the body in various ways. The steam pits, application of hot mud over the body; the use of natural hot springs, etc., were traditional remedies for many ills; and before judging this primitive therapy as whims of Indian imagination, note the modern clinics and physicians administering hot water treatments, steam baths, hot mud plasters, electric heat and numerous other steam heat applications.

The more we become involved in the lives of our Indian predecessors, the more we find that the white man has adopted to his use many, many things inspired by those native people. Herbal remedies, names, recognition of a spiritual appeasement, the fate of oppressed freedom, the slow healing of broken trust, natural food preparation and other Indian lore are but a few of the thought provoking things found in our great Indian heritage.

The natives of our land, though repeatedly misled, misunderstood and forced into submission, have magnificently survived the transformation from the wild, free life to that of an American society of equal rights and citizenry. It has been my personal lot to have maintained throughout my life a meaningful respect for our Indian blood.

Ancient Crude Work Discovery

The early Stone Age work pictured in Figs. 144 to 147, inclusive, are part of a recent discovery in Jackson County, Oregon. The work is very primitive in nature, and made from varying shades of the jasper stone. No fine flaking was in evidence at this site, all pieces being formed by the percussion method. Thousands of rough stone edges had apparently been spawled off and examined for suitable pieces to work into the desired points, axes, knives, etc. Many pieces are so crude that evidently rock collectors have not yet recognized the touch by human hands.

There are indications of former earth disruption in the area; volcanic action. Jasper is fused into lava formations and many of these show where the aborigine has broken the jasper out of lava boulders. He was undoubtedly attracted to this deposit by the beautiful display of colored stone ranging from pure red, yellow, green, brown and various intermixed shades. Deep creek channels have dislodged many fine specimens that were found around and under bedrock boulders.

My family and I have gathered nearly one hundred pieces of the ancient work. After sorting out the blanks, cleaning up and displaying them side by side, it is easy to identify the purpose for which each was made. From all things observed at this site, indications are that the work was done by a wandering tribe of aborigine; most probably in the second stage or Archaic period of approximately 5000 years B.C. This is the conclusion of advanced scholars in the field, taking into consideration the relationship to the Crater Lake eruption, which was just short of 5000 B.C. If these deductions are correct, (which we have no reasons to disbelieve) the discovery is one of the oldest found on western slopes of the Oregon Cascades.

Locating Habitation Sites

As a reassessment of important things to observe in locating a permanent site of habitation, a few reminders are in order. At the confluence of two streams large enough to carry steelhead and salmon runs, the Indian found a natural location to his advantage; as did he at falls and spawning grounds.

In mountainous areas, we look for a source of water such as springs, creeks or seepage spots. Many springs are now sluffed in or covered with sod growth. I have dug out seepage spots, and found in two of them nice little rocked-up wells that, upon cleaning out, let the water trickle once again over the top.

Pacific shell mounds may now be covered with brush, grass, sand and dust accumulation, but a few test trenches starting at ground level will determine if they are a natural dirt knoll or a deep shell buildup.

The vast Oregon Desert is at present an exception, but we are reminded of the period when it was under the waters of an inland sea. Chapter 1 has dealt fully with present day conditions and local spots of interest to collectors.

In all cases a survey must be made of the terrain. Endeavor to associate yourself with existing conditions that the Indian may have seen before the changes brought on by centuries of erosion or buildups. From this point on, it is entirely up to the collector to investigate further.

Make an assessment of things found to determining whether or not to proceed with a thorough excavation. We at present have a great opportunity to confirm and reassess the all important factor of ground formation on the upper banks of Rogue River. The sedimentary sand, gravel, volcanic ash and granulated pumice layers are giving us the ancient story possibly equal to, and in some instances more accurate than carbon dating, where the material could be contaminated. There is no disputing those pumice and volcanic ash deposits blown from the Crater Lake eruption of 5,600 B.C.; thin in places, heavy in others and found from a few inches beneath the present surface to several feet deep, according to river fills and cutting action. We are fortunate in this section of the Cascade Range to have an accurate time table set by that great volcanic eruption. Whatever the geological features, we are most interested in the tangible evidence of human existence during and prior to the falling of voluminous clouds of pumice and ash. This comes in various forms; fire broken rock, crude metates, campfire charcoal, an occasional arrow point or perhaps a segment of bone needle showing the work of a human hand.

Tepee Rings

The foregoing chapters have dealt quite fully with the Indian's regional environments, and many susceptible theories put under heavy strain by tangible discoveries; one of which springs from the native tepee ring. Through a growing public interest in this subject, I find it in keeping to relate a personal experience.

Former experiences have shown that deviations from a logical course you may be pursuing are often necessary to coincide with the primitive's trend of thinking. This should come naturally as underground work progresses; unless those involved are so preoccupied with a certain line of findings that they are reluctant to taper off and scout the area for possible new leads.

The value of flexibility is seen in a 1971 project my family and I experienced on the western Cascade slopes in Jackson County, Oregon. We had on many occasions dug and screened the ridge for lost or scattered points, which usually netted a half dozen to twenty in a day. The area was a perfect location, with the wind breaks good, spring water plentiful and in the midst of game country. Still no evidence of a permanent campsite was found. Intermittent surveys were made for any indication of a camp. Surface irregularities were inspected, and especially any sign of prehistoric ground disturbance.

All seemed of no avail, when after a long day's screening and within a few feet of our digging a shallow, neatly circular depression of perhaps twenty feet in diameter was detected under the sod, brush growth and second growth trees. This could be a tepee dugout site; possibly the one from which the surrounding points had originated. A followup trip was then planned.

A rotted tree stump sink was ruled out, after a deep center hole revealed a much used, rocked-up firepit. Erosion had filled the spot to nearly surface level, but there was no doubt now that this was an ancient tepee ring. Without question, time and the elements had all but defaced the last visible signs of this old dwelling site.

Uncovering was begun in two directions, (on the firepit level) which revealed a neatly constructed rock wall, approximately two and one half feet high around the outer perimeter. This wall was made much the same as we would lay bricks.

There were intervening spaces between the large rock slabs. These crevices are prospective niches for tribal layaways. Troweling seeped in dirt from the one time voids, and removing wall rock was continued until, (to our delight) sixty some points came sliding down. We held steadfast to this system, which netted us over one hundred fine artifacts. The two skinning knives, stone and bone punches, a pair of stone earrings, spearheads, a human effigy engraving and numerous arrowheads, constituted the fascinating find. An item worthy of speculation was found on the back floor level. A layer of fine, rich, dark dirt mixture indicated the remains of a pile of decomposed fibrous bedding, or possibly fur robes.

The amazing part of this discovery lies not in the artifacts themselves; for they are of wide distribution. The method of discovery should register noticeably in the minds of future collectors. Ground sample tracing here was nearly impossible, for the ancient tepee area had been walked over, its surface distorted; dug and screened around for twenty years by various groups. Such conditions are often signs of concentrated findings by previous hunters.

The above surface tepee ring is simply the circular remains of a dirt raise around the onetime tepee floor, to provide a watershed and warmth retainer.

My attention has primarily been centered on the northwest sites due to personal contacts and involvement in the search for overlooked artifacts. Those explored in the Montana-(south) Dakota-(northern)-Wyoming areas run closely true to form with those explored in farther west regions to and beyond the Cascade Range.

These plainly visible rings usually produce little more than bone segments, ash and charcoal, chipping spawls and possibly a few good points intermingled with broken ones. This has been my experience. However, a substantial one urges us to put forth greater effort to locate the more ancient, richer ring sites that have slackened and weathered down to or below the original surface.

To supplement our knowledge of construction, locations and tribal styling of tepees, wigwams, wickiups, hogans and other forms of native dwelling shelters, many Indian history writers have dealt well with this subject. One publication highly recommended (and available at prominent book shops) is the book, The American Indian, an Oliver LaFarge Pictorial History Production—third printing 1966, Library of Congress card number: 60-14881.

Lost Creek Dam

At present this mile long, secondary rise from the river frontage is being worked by the State's scientific personnel; but without doubt many small areas will never be touched before being lost under the water of the Lost Creek dam, now under construction. Here, as in most locations, the first findings were made by individuals; then taken over by archaeologists, posted and out of bounds to all others.

Such action is very necessary in exploring the primitive habitations, but it does serve to widen the breach between State interests and the finder. My personal opinion is that many fine sites would not be kept hush-hush if a more cooperative system were worked out. For instance, issue a permit to the capable amateur to work bypassed spots alongside and under the supervision of the State's people. He is going to continue his relic search with or without training, anyway, so why not give the issue deep consideration?

Bring It In

Any stone bearing signs of human work should be brought in when found; whether appearing worn out, crude or broken. The most inconspicuous looking segment could provide an important link to broken trails in prehistoric migrations. Amateur collectors, hobbyists, recreationists or any outdoorsmen should keep this in mind, as well as any archaeological society. To be sure of its possible importance, bring it in.

Conclusion

There have been no monetary gains from my collection, nor has any grant been extended toward field operations. Only from personal interest have all things possible from my findings been recorded, in complying to archaeological research standards. Therefore, I believe it clearly seen that my personal efforts and time involved have been solely to preserve and display the works of our predecessors. There is no historical outlet from a private relic box. The future generations have a right to Stone Age knowledge.

The final tabulation of things found, (related within the bounds of self limitation) may be less impressive than the same disposition made through archaeological bulletins. Nevertheless, my findings should expand the sphere of research capabilities. Personal experiences have come with the years; discoveries have exceeded my wildest expectations.

An open mind welcomes constructive differences of opinion, and appreciates diversified viewpoints pertaining to the primitive works. Branching theories and speculations are strengthening factors to a writing; thoroughly within the individual's right. One encounters a different approach to the mountain peak from each of its four sides, yet all terminate at the same crest.

Silent Arrows will hopefully promote deeper penetrations into primitive territories; whether on a hobby basis, through scientific involvement, or simply because of a personal ambition to trace a hereditary lineage. I find the work to be invigorating, educational and a wholesome outlet for pentup energies.

In conclusion I wish to express my sincere gratitude to the good people who helped me fulfill the ambitions of a personal career. I am deeply indebted to those who gladly gave permission to explore on their premises; the oldtimers who shared their cabin and an invitation to sit at the table; and friends who occasionally donated an artifact. Especially did I feel that goodwill atmosphere of western hospitality surrounding a stranger.

I cherish the memory of those grand old Indians, most of them departed now, who unboastingly and without reservation related to me a volume of information on early Indian life; their customs, traits, cultures and always the longing for their former freedom in the open spaces. Those impressive and educational friend to friend talks were instrumental in laying the foundation issues for this book.

I thank the members of my entire family for their willing hands, efforts and moral support in helping me to achieve the goal of my seventy years ambition; a meaningful collection of Indian history and their Stone Age cultures. I extend to them my very special appreciation.

Last but not least, I am grateful for the protective hand of Providence on lone and hazardous explorations into crumbling caves, under precipitous canyon walls and over burning, shifting sanddune spaces dancing with tricky mirages.

Should the questions be asked, "Has it been worth it all? Would you do it all over again?" my answer would be, "Hand me a pick and shovel, load up the packsack, and set the alarm for 3:30 A.M."

Beyond the Embers

Beside the trail, I lay one night
  Screening thoughts through drousing mind,
As embers softened and cooled till morn
  To flame anew in pre-dawn light.

It seems the plans are made and done,
  Through mist we see at times,
And say we yes or say we no,
  All worldly trails lead to but one.

The Great Creator under Heaven's hue,
  Through nature's balm on wound and scar
In mystic life all 'round, has
  Challenged the old by birth of new.

Today a stately, towering pine,
  Swaying in nature's bosom of sun,
Lays down tomorrow to bed the new,
  So willed and planned by passing time.

Winter doth blanket to nurse the spring,
  The sun must set to rise again,
Trails are dimmed by autumn cover,
  But new leaves await the bird on wing.

The heart is bruised by Earthly mete,
  Losses borne, we know not why,
But comes the light and reward is high,
  One day, There, when God we meet.

                         Earl F. Moore

BIBLIOGRAPHY

American Indian, The. Oliver LaFarge Pictorial Production Guide to Understanding Idaho Archaeology by Robert Butler. Idaho State University Museum.

Indian and Eskimo Artifacts of North America by Charles Miles. Crown Publisher, Bonanza Books, N. Y.

Indians of the United States by Dr. Clark Wissler. Doubleday.

My Friend, the Indian by Colonel James McLaughlin. Houghton-Mifflin.

ACKNOWLEDGMENTS AND CREDITS

Brainerd, Max
Brown, Archie
Brown, Mrs..Amelia
Butler, Robert
Cressman, Dr. L. S.
Edwards, Herb and Yvonne
Evans, Arthur
Greb, Darrell and Nadra
Griffin, Mr. and Mrs. Seeley
Haddenham, D. C.
Hittle, Mr. and Mrs. William
Indian Pete
Jaynes, Francis
Long, Rueb

Mapel, Charles and June
Mays, Nellie
McDonald, Rosie
Miles, Charles
Schaub, Richard
Swanson, Dr. Earl H.
Tall Jim
Thompson, Flora
Thompson, Henry
Thompson, Tommy
Tiny
Von der Hellen, Mr. William
Wissler, Dr. Clark
Woodward, Arthur

PHOTO CREDITS

James Anders, Ander's Studio, Medford, Oregon
Juanita Anderson, Medford, Oregon
Herb Edwards, Central Point, Oregon
Ken Knusted, Central Point, Oregon
Earl Moore, Central Point, Oregon

ILLUSTRATIONS INDEX

Original Sketches and Paintings by Juanita Anderson

PHOTOGRAPHS

STORIES INDEX

REFERENCE INDEX

INDEX (continued)